BAD SHAMAN BLUES

Books by W.N. Herbert

POETRY

Sterts & Stobies, with Robert Crawford (Obog Books, 1985)
Sharawaggi, with Robert Crawford (Polygon, 1990)
Dundee Doldrums (Galliard, 1991)
Anither Music (Vennel Press, 1991)
The Testament of the Reverend Thomas Dick (Arc Publications, 1994)
Forked Tongue (Bloodaxe Books, 1994)
Cabaret McGonagall (Bloodaxe Books, 1996)
The Laurelude (Bloodaxe Books, 1998)
The Big Bumper Book of Troy (Bloodaxe Books, 2002)
Bad Shaman Blues (Bloodaxe Books, 2006)

LITERARY CRITICISM

To Circumjack MacDiarmid (Oxford University Press, 1992)
Strong Words: modern poets on modern poetry
   edited with Matthew Hollis (Bloodaxe Books, 2000)

BAD SHAMAN BLUES

W.N. HERBERT

BLOODAXE BOOKS

ISBN: 1 85224 728 2

First published 2006 by
Bloodaxe Books Ltd,
Highgreen,
Tarset,
Northumberland NE48 1RP.

www.bloodaxebooks.com
For further information about Bloodaxe titles
please visit our website or write to
the above address for a catalogue.

Bloodaxe Books Ltd acknowledges
the financial assistance of
Arts Council England, North East.

Cover printing by J. Thomson Colour Printers Ltd, Glasgow.

Printed in Great Britain by
Bell & Bain Limited, Glasgow, Scotland.

...the Khant saw the world in minutely observed physical detail, like a precise but perspectiveless scientific drawing. For example, they had no words that translated as 'bird' or 'fish', only words for specific species. Eighty per cent of their vocabulary consisted of verbs – there were different ones for 'sitting on a log', 'sitting on a stump' and 'sitting on the ground' – and they possessed an extraordinary range of terms to do with sound. 'The noise a bear makes walking through cranberry bushes' had its own word, as did 'the noise a duck makes landing quietly on water'. Abstract nouns were few...The word for 'photograph' literally translated as 'a pool of still water'...

ANNA REID, *The Shaman's Coat*

CONTENTS

GEORGIOUPOLICS

OVER THE WALL   I

the drowned landscape is here
in the dark the separated
　　　lonely hanging step is here

YANG LIAN

Farewell to La Gazzetta

While you cling to your thirties you're deluded
    you're linked to ageing gods: those goods
with seasons still to play: Signori, Zola...
    (you'd neither score nor save their goals).
Their sprint towards retirement finds you clinging
    to truthless youth, but here's the thing:
since Channel Four has hacked the whole peninsu-
    la from their schedules, that sick prince
called your illusion dies here. Greet those forties
    with fortitude, or greet and snort.

Time sneers at our retorts to rampant ageing –
    our midlife Harley's farting rage.
So say farewell to all pretence at manhood:
    the ninety-minute legs, the tan
that once looked buff, not tangerine; be careful
    combing decockatoodled hair.
Farewell to your surprising young erections,
    the corncob midriff. Genuflect
before the set that's emptied of your icons
    and board the bastard fitness-bike.

Farewell to teams for which I half-screamed *Forza!*
    dreaming they got my full support:
to Lazio's most fascistic of tifosi,
    miles from my left-winged repose.
Sofad each Sunday with a cold Peroni
    I was the phony on the phone
trying to win a ticket to Bologna
    but if I had, would I have gone?
I put my maleness in another country
    where I need never meet the runt.

Goodbye to all the players that the ratings
     decided we can't watch: the blate,
the mediocre, the great but bloody luckless,
     and those who never gave a fuck.
Goodbye to Battistuta and Gattuso;
     Maldini, Nedved – hear my blues –
to Rui Costa, Cannavaro, Nesta,
     Morfeo, Buffon; and the best
presenter, pun-drenched alter ego, boyish
     balding James Richardson, goodbye.

Schwitters in Ambleside

You would expect the vestiges of chaos
to accompany him to his alien grave,
instead this sheepish town contents itself
with making little headstones out of slate.
Cramped, stubby, but free-standing: all this grey was
some use, one way of shaping sense, relief
for eyes from lifting to hills filled with life-
lessness, the way at Honister you pass

onto the scree slopes of some outer moon
they had no image for back when he came
to colonise the idea of his death.
To settle where they couldn't gauge his worth,
to build the wall that sealed him off from fame,
to tear himself off and stick his self down.

Over the Wall

1

When you drive the road that cuts to Carlisle
year-long, from week to week in parallel
to that constrictor's vertebrae, the Wall;
from its disjointed jaws that try to swallow
all the Tyne like a gazelle, past
old Cuddy's Crags, the Whin Sill;
glancing north to where in autumn and in evening
the light begins to strip the local greens away
in favour of a brittle ochre hue –
you start to feel the Romans got the border right.

2

True Wall, magnetic Wall,
Wall that never mentions North
but hints obliquely like an only line:
here begins beyond.

Here all thought of borders was born
to the west of empire,
swaddled in vallum and cribbed with stone,
where before they had let their sense of limits
seep through the babble:
horribilesque ultimosque Britannos

Here men began to hold the shrinking world
that had held them
upon her unbound breasts.

3

You start to think it's like a mirror
that you somehow escaped through with
a book held in your trailing hand
that sticks in the liminal air as though across bars.

You want to plead, 'O wall,
O sweet and lovely wall,
through whom I see my bliss, let all

my drag of luggage pass,' until,
spine first, high as hawks, the book begins to appear,
steadying there at the end of your kitestring arm.

The difficult words can't make it through,
their letters swoop and clatter in the grass like armour;
their questions fall on the other side
of the unguarded Wall, their great marks sprawl
untranslated in the barbaric grass:
armis/ reddidit aeratis sonitum

Border Cow

A cow is pissing in the twilight:
a black cow, in a field of brown and white
sisters, looking across the hills
to the border, though she doesn't know this.
She has a cord that runs along her back
which something has seized abruptly,
rodding her tail up, runkling her neck.

Her stream gleams thickly as
the air gains evening's soot-smuts:
it strings her to the grass
at a strict angle, no curve,
just the liquid she leans against
gleaming like a narwhal's tusk, an ashplant,
as she strains to be relieved.

dis manibus

when all scrolls fail
and what survives of script
is chiselled on graves

when stone is stolen
and bones lose names
we're only, wholly here

our spirits deify
this landscape by
departing into it

our spirits defy
the glutting flow
and hide in glimpses

momentary fanes,
this cult of peripherals, where
gliff must stand for glyph

an alphabet of tracks:
claws and soles
hooves and paws

parochial recoveries:
the dialect of touch
the elegies of water

Sideling Hieroglyphics

The hawk that shears the hedge then steadies, held
above the verge by urgent need, he is
old Egypt's silhouette, the pictogram
for 'kill'. There is a lock to which he is
continually the key that must release
a narrow death from everywhere in air.
He is the tender axe that has to fall.

Haltwhistle Burn

Land Rovers mush up and whippets mince in
the leaves in the lane. The firework committee
is setting up their PA in a field
where bin-liners hang from poles and a tractor
shoves the ribs of furniture and pallets
into a mound. That bass motif is replaced
by a swell of Grieg as I walk by the burn
darkened in spate. Buttery knives of light
push through the trees and the rain begins
to hold off beginning. Halfway to
the Roman Wall there is a pipe-gush
that stains the opposite bank, its weed-
lined dry-stone, with mad-foam lardy trails.
And somewhere underneath that is a pool
or boulder that the streaming glugs through
or over, a bouncing glottal note that's like
a distant murmur on some night radio,
the set not tuned in properly but still
aligned to that submerged discourse. A tone
that survives whatever language it might feed on
like flame; a voice addressing us where we sleep
and do not know we're being spoken to.
It tells us who we are and what we do.

Song of the Shieldsmen

From Merzbau to Mithraeum
we march along this wall:
if we saw Picts we'd slay them
but Picts are bloody small.

They've got into our bloodstream
they've got inside our heads,
we think we're pigging Latin
we're pigging Picts instead.

There's Pictish on our bus tickets
there's Pict yeast in our bread,
and when we march upon this wall
there's Picts climb in our beds.

Our sperms have nanoPicts attached
that leap onto our eggs,
and when we march through marshy grass
we've leech-Picts on our legs.

A Pict is everything we hate
because we've never known:
from Dada art to the feel of Fate,
a Pict's what we can't own.

A Pict's the thing that lives upon
the tongue-tip of our doubt,
a Pict's the virus of our dreams
we drown out with this shout:

From Mithraeum to Merzbau
we fear they will attack,
so when we've marched from there to here
we turn and march right back.

The Hoppings

Time to run the futures' gauntlet, between
the fortune-tellers' Alice-banded caravans,
that open croc jaw pegged with wooden teeth
which promise to unsheathe your only truth,
the way their signs assure you of descent
from one prognosticator's faultless descant.

Each one must brew the facts from scattered fates
like rain impelled into neat glassy beads
between the petals of her brain. Walk on
through scent collisions – candy and adrenaline –
the airbrushed purple mouths on waltzers,
the horses grinning at the wurlitzer,
nearly extinct, this conjured hysterical shake
of all our children's sugared vertebrae.

But you're still reading from her freckled back,
that woman, strapless on a mattress, slack
outside a pair of mobile homes once seen
cornered with horses on a municipal green.
Heading for the helter skelter, you want to know
the one sharp life which she would not have told.

A Fane (M167)

The glare before the Jesmond flyover
gets cut off by the concrete as I drive
into a kind of temple listening
to Josquin's Missa 'Pange lingua', past
unfluted columns and the flanking slopes
that beam a lime tone through the slim young trees.

Their stunted canopies are hidden by
this slabbed and sodium-lit darkness where
that stir of voices, first heard in Ferrara
in the sixteenth century, is brushed
by quiet crackles like a censer's swish.

We all rush in and no one wants to linger –
pause in neutral genuflection at
the bollard, or just speed through the ritual:
look signal and manoeuvre. Then we try
to leave but jam into the exit lanes
emerging from the shade.

                   The curving lip
of the ascending ramp has crumbled so
a constant drip of water can be caught
in the sunlight. We see it and we don't.

Counting Magpies in Newcastle

Goodmorrow mister magpie, how's your mate?

In Donegal the drivers know
each other and the sheepgut roads
too well to wave. They don't know me,
but spot my father's local plates
and lift a finger from the wheel.

That smallest gesture's hard to do
down streets you don't belong to, like
North Tyneside's: on the Coast Road's length
I find I've grown adept instead
at recognising magpies' flight.

White bellies dip across the lanes
as though despairing that they'll reach
each leafless lamppost opposite;
black archeopteryxes' tails
sustain them till they perch and flick.

I feel the shiftless need to count
and must acknowledge singletons –
just one's too yang, too odd, too male –
enquire about his absent mate,
placate polarities for luck.

I downplay this compulsion when
a passenger might notice: mute
the mantra, and, still searching for
that female by default, I lift
a casual-looking fingertip.

Shields Moon

As Eh wiz waulkin hame frae work
a reid mune kythed abune thi lang sea waa
atween thi statue o Collingwood
white as aa thi maas
squallochin i thi Gut
and thi lichthoose blintin at thi mou o thi firth.

And she wiz lyk a rosy whulk,
an ammonite wi nae
feegaries o clood aboot ur,
no fauch aboot thi fiss
but thi orange o a weelraked coal.

And Eh wiz caucht atween
thi heid oan a Guinness at thi Doll
an thi fizzog on a Creamola bowl, thon tosie
E-number-lumbert pudden
meh gran stirred jeely in –

Till a stertlin o thi gulls
skellit oan thi clood o ma mind
iconic bluid fae a pelican's breist,
and doon thi wame o meh ain hoose
thi lichts bleezed oot thi mune's semm glim:
lyk a mither's flow that ceases as
hir dochtir's draught begins,

thi auld mune geein wey
tae thi wean ut's cairried
in its aefauld airms.

kythed: revealed; *squallochin:* crying out shrilly; *blintin:* glancing; *feegaries:* fineries
in dress; *fauch:* pale, yellowish; *tosie:* cosy, flushed; *maas:* gulls; *skellit:* spilt;
aefauld: faithful, single-minded.

A Midsummer Light's Nighthouse

1

In Winter the Old High Light speaks
the language of the sea winds
and the hail: cold unwraps itself, sheet
after sheet, around its weeping edge.

In the spring it rediscovers sunlight,
lets the clouds peel off like gulls
from its lead-lidded eyeball. The earth wind mouths
against the landing door, yammering and keen.

But in the simmer-dim and dark it talks
in its own dialect: sudden as a stairwell
and silent as a corridor when the light-switch
flicks, it tells me how to listen.

2

Where do you think the music comes up from,
manifested in the taut ropes ringing
off masts of fishing boats, the grunt of motors rippling
like a fat moon's dribble on the river
and the knocking tread that's boxes, dropped upon the quays?

Where do you think the music groups itself
before the year turns over in the night?
It's propped against these timbers like a giant lens;
it's like a sunfish that's warmed itself in top waters
the eye flashing as it rolls away and drops.

3

It is by how we translate silence that
the dead become retongued = listen to
this empty air that fills two centuries
and more of chamber with the dreaming crush
of families: how it holds the creases in
their faces; how it's poised between their breaths.

4

Let the admiral slither from
his pedestal, turned from guanoed marble to
white walrus, a crawling beluga,
and pipe in his ship-whistle voice canary songs
of old calamities, wars dissolving on water.

Let the smuggler woman come
in her jellyfish petticoats, ribbons fouled with sons,
smearing the walls with rum-thickened venom,
and slur in old tobacco tones her press-gang blues,
her welcoming couplets like cold thighs.

5

The sea does not bring forth in autumn
like an orchard – it draws back
like a page that's pinched for turning.
We read in it abeyance, not a swell.

Therefore the mind exerts its right
to halt the story, poise us on this sill
before the river sweeps the chimes away
and buries yet another solstice out at sea.

These other lives that surged before us,
let them be the gap before this midnight's tick:
our own no more inhabitable void succeeds it,
and the High Light is our common home.

Antinous of the Tyne

Ignore the statues. Here we have you,
floating face down, not searching Tyne
    for divinity,
      not looking at all,
just floating that marble-firm backside,
   those white thighs splayed in brown.

You died in Egypt, in that huge gap
between the facts called intimacy
    or perhaps the Nile,
      so what's washed you here
beneath our noses at Arbeia
   must be a myth like love.

Some crocodile's flung your guts around
before you got here, or the fingers
    of Hadrian have
      sought out soft omens
caresses couldn't yield, that you'd pass
   passion's liquid thresholds.

Your curls are drenched in more than perfume
and your lips pout with a darker stain,
    a greater vintage
      makes your cheeks hectic
than the supply ship brings: you've joined those
   the gods are sorry died.

Osiris, Dionysus, Hermes:
your soul was told to dwell with them, by
    your emperor, in
      a glut of temples,
a cult flowing like a river past
   the waiting banks of faith.

Those unreflective shores, anxious to
observe their latest rites whether you
     wept into silks with
     joy or not, ageing
with the hard breath of your master on
   your nape, not twenty yet.

Ignore the statues that piece your moods
together, like a mosaic they tramped
     upon for decades:
     concentrate on coins
that hold your godhead, still in the mouths
   of Danube, Tyne, like teats.

Tyne Tunnel

These days I tune in specially
as I approach the tunnel, hoping for
sopranos, pianistic flourishes,
colouristic passages, as I pay and wind
my window up, switch on dipped lights
and descend to the river's underbelly.

The static comes in swells, quite leisurely:
it pulls itself over the voice, the strings,
it shushes, couries, smothers, sinks,
and then it reigns like poison in the lug,
a crush of other traffic, a scrape and drag –
cans across rock, silt through gills: the gully.

I always feel it will be troubled by
some voice that breaks in with a song
you only hear down here: the tongue
compressed, half-ham, half-Janacek;
the message cold, eruptive, wrecked –
but there's nothing till sunlight and, gradually,

the same tune altered by the weight of water.

Zamyatin in Heaton

conceived of Jesmond as the icy keel
of class conformity, and laid it down;
here English bergs cut scones with stainless steel,
sank tea Titanics, watched each other drown –
a quaker Archangel of publessness
where vicars trapped their dicks in sharp routines.
He saw that fear of flesh, of hope, of mess,
made people turn themselves into machines,
and realised the Revolution's grip
on its own *muzhiks'* soft interior gears
was also prudish, crude, mechanical;
just as the top Range Rovers brusquely slip
down Acorn Road today, it crushed its fears,
since what it couldn't measure it could kill.

For Andrew Waterhouse

For the good are always the merry
Save by an evil chance

W.B. YEATS
'The Fiddler of Dooney'

An Irish reel is in my ears
    not one of yours;
Northumberland has rival airs,
but that was what they played
the night I heard: *The Sligo Maid* –
    strange what endures.

Displacement is our theme of themes,
    it's what remains:
the way we can't remember dreams
that still, like partial songs, affect
the unmelodic intellect
    and tune our brains.

So poets from the splintered North
    have made roots here:
from south of Humber, past the Forth,
come settler saplings slow to bear
the fruit and leaves that feed the air
    if granted years.

And that was what you couldn't give
    your own songs' book,
the music's womb that wants to live
no matter what your mind may feel:
we write laments for all the reels
    that your hand took.

But what I mourn here more's the friend
    who died so friendless,
for no one could prevent that end
but you, displaced completely from
our love, your art – you needed numb-
    ness to be endless.

The fiddler's first above, says Yeats –
        let us abjure
all music past those pearl-stuck gates:
the breath inside a single air
is worth all Heaven's atmosphere –
        yet can't endure.

Bar Mirror Variations

Mirror bar is empty, no matter how
merry the bottleboys in unreflective here.
Mirror bar is silent, no matter how
heated the geekboys' PC game debates.
Mirror bar displays the roof of its placid mouth
and swallows up our loudest lager choir.

Not even I can sit there though I care
enough to chart its changeless weather
through the evolution of Saturdays,
the transitions here from three o'clock
kick-off in the languageless forest of pints
to five's lighting of the testosterone lamps.

While cack tacticians roar I envisage
the empty seats and glassless tables that
the mirrors' angles cannot show; imagine
the deserted streets of Mirrortoon, always
just evacuated, that whole island now restored
by mere silvering to an undemolished whole.

Our constant past still haunts those heights
of tarnishing and soon-to-exit portals
while we desocialised ones sit and try
to shuffle invalid papers into shape out here,
knowing that old official face who mediates
the one transition we're too scared to make.

LOST FILMS

All our understanding of ancient Greek [statues] is based on copies. Maybe our understanding of the world is also based on copies. On copies and translations. So they are not the real thing, they are something that has changed. So for me, in this sense, the fake things also have a great meaning. We are born to read a fake world.

XI CHUAN

I shall get up and dance with my own shadow

SU SHI

The Wall at Huanghua

It never once occurred to me I'd stepped
beyond the Wall into that space which might
have corresponded with my own uncivil turf.
My sympathies were all with that commander
who built this plunging stretch to such high specs
that the expense led to his execution:
three days his torso stood, refusing to
accept its head had been removed, until
accounts came back of no corruption, and,
his legacy still standing, it lay down,
gave its consent to be entombed. We parked
past tables piled with T-shirts, peanuts, cards,
and past that sign, 'The Great Wall closeo
for reconstruction' – took our laughing snaps,
and then returned from outerness onto
the little modern dam that linked two parts
which slither madly for green mohair heights,
make dragons' backbones that I'd thought were just
abrupt on scrolls. I made to cross its nerve
until stopped by a homemade MRL
of fireworks that one woman tried to charge
for lighting. We retreated to a bridge
so highly-sprung its timbers bounced us off
upon a rushing café owner's porch.
It took six yuan each to get us off
and start the climb towards a patch of Wall
that wasn't being quite so much rebuilt.

And then the steam horizon sank to stems,
the coils of stone shrank to a worm cast path
traversing hips and collarbones of fields
beneath a green fir fuzz, among the fruit
that none of us could name. And then we found
upon a backless legless chair a gran
thrusting a card which told us that to cross
the unseen borders of her land would cost
three yuan. And when we'd all paid, she smiled
and said what could have been 'Huanghua', and waved
her tiny hands as though to draw us in.

But we climbed on, although the path was now
so steep I had to pause for Pascale or
for breath, and glancing at my feet for balance
saw a brief line of reddish-orange ants,
and, as I watched, one stumbled in mid-climb.
By now we could hear singing from above,
so at a fork we took the transverse path
to reach the battlements and dodge the drunks.

But as we cut across and neared the Wall
events began converging at the point
I realised my left foot would soon occupy
as I grabbed at a coping-stone and swung:
the singers shifted to a warning shout;
a man ran down the Wall's sheer top to wave
his red arm-banded arm attempting to
prevent the contact I had barely made
as rain commenced to pelting all our faces.
We fell back, drenched in seconds, seeking out
the shelter of those unknown trees, still on
the ancient side of home, and as the path
dissolved beneath us, made out figures on
the opposite stretch strolling up and down
beneath umbrellas. And so we scramble-fell
back past the chair-seat where we had been warned,
and tramped across the trampolining bridge
in a grim line, then climbed up to collapse –
just as the rain stopped – in a restaurant
beneath a route up to the Wall that made
our shattered legs and bellies call for lunch.

And here we sat and drank ourselves back dry
on *chá* and *píjiŭ*, failing to pronounce
the simplest nouns for food, until our drivers
collapsed at our inept impersonations of
zhūròu, its snout still grunting in the bowl,
jīròu puck-pucking after being broiled,
and ordered for us all. As donkeys passed
with brand new wall stones slung across their backs,
I paid a visit to the final resting place
of the best bowel in China's finest work,
then once more tested which way my knees bent,

until the half of us still mobile stood
upon the tumbled pavement of the Wall
and looked out through a mile-fort's window at
the crazy snake of limits cresting hills
that no foe with a scrap of armour in
this heat or still worse snow would think to scale –
as though the crushing waves of milliards
of centuries of rock-face could be crowned
or chained. As though this border where we lean
between the two not being heres – before as
endless as after – could be frozen, kept
out of those calculations we still hope
do not apply to us. This thought is what
we wish so much to cordon off we stitch
these scars across the planet's torso for
the moon-hare to stare down on: what the Wall
keeps out is seamed to that which it keeps in
so intimately that the only way
to tell the two apart is by this step
we take unknowingly across its brink
or back. I looked across at nothing through
the window in the roofless fort, my head
refusing for the moment to depart
my shoulders, then descended to my friends
and left the brittle border for Beijing.

Forbidden

We approach everything from the north;
pass the Tower of Concentric Corners
which appeared to an emperor in the dream,
and pause in a swelter before the wrong gate.
Here beneath Coal Mountain you can hear
old people practice their hanging notes, where
a fleeing emperor chose to tie a noose.

Brushing the brass nodules on the door
purchasing the chemically cleansed water
declining the commentary of Roger Moore,
I step over the first of the many thresholds
as though here liminality knew no limits,
introversion found no final atom –
and enter the Forbidden City.

The Hill of Accumulated Beauty
is all the well-holed rocks they could gather
interlocking to form a drab scramble –
too many eyes can rub away exquisiteness.
Lady, the four slow-growing junipers
were split at their roots to form the forked legs
of the character *rén*, meaning 'man'.

Among the rocks twisting on their pedestals
I photograph Lian where his father stood
back from the ageing farm for intellectuals:
he rewrites the ghost of that bare pose
with his bones' long quills, and the lens can't see
inside his chest, in this moment of exposure,
blood stamp the character for 'heart'.

Because we have entered from the north
I see everything from an emperor's perspective
following his perineal cloud and dragon path
through small pavilions to opening
and opening courtyards like the opposite
of a voice, growing louder and louder
until the world shakes to pieces.

The City is continually being cleft
into dragon and phoenix, Mandarin and Manchurian
on the signs above the expanding palaces.
Male and female join along a scar
of perspiration until we enter the tiny room
where policies were forged, where an emperor failed
to shake you out of the dream

more intimate than his private chambers
where concubines were swaddled in saffron
and carried like larvae to the breeding bed,
eunuchs noting future rulers' mothers
the way we film his furniture through glass.
The pedestal for an absent lion holds
its imprint of rump and paws, inch-deep with rain.

From here on out the courtyards swell,
pavilions shun the drowsy emissaries
performing their duties to curiosity.
Places of examination, proclamation and execution
release order into the squatting heavens.
Little troops of police begin to march
as we pass beyond the entrance barrier.

People without feet line our way,
caps out or hands if they have them.
A small old man smiles and takes the plastic bottle
I bought on the way in, crumples it and walks off
as we reawaken to how hot it is, how crowded,
how alone it felt in there, in the dream
where something could not be said.

And fighting against the stream in the tunnel
we pass below the giant face of Mao
one eye occupying the west and one the east;
and like it look upon Tiananmen,
its vastness as the City's would-be twin.
It's June the 4th, sixteen years on,
and it's barely occupied at all.

Three Lost Films

1

The cube-shaped theatre building in the temple grounds at Penglai: a small building where we'd crowded into a ground floor room to watch this continuously rotating video of the mirage phenomenon seen out at sea from this spot for thousands of years. The video is from three or four years ago, not very good quality, and it shows excited crowds on the seaward ramparts. The temple complex is quite high above the sea on cliffs it follows with a restraining rampart but otherwise crowds up to at all angles, so when the camera pans there are constant profiles of curving roofs with their green tiles and rows of mythical beasts on the eaves, each following a combination first seen in the Forbidden City: eagles and dragons and a triceratops-like creature, and lastly a figure on a horse the locals call 'No Hope'. All the heads of all the witnesses (and apparently the dragon-beasts, who must have seen all this before) are looking out to sea and whooping with a genuine surprise.

The camera keeps turning to what looks like ink or sand pouring from an invisible tray into the sea in horizontally distended hour-glass shapes you gradually grasp are huge. Whoops continue as these separate out and form three colossal shapes and you remember the conversation with Lian on the night bus to Wansongpu: the three floating mountains of the gods of Taoist legend. Supposedly a voyage in search of these islands that ended up discovering Japan. Then the camera cuts uselessly back to the faces by the Puzhao light tower. They're still attempting to control their sense of the random luck of this happening now and their surprise, because they do seem to be wondering how this thing works – it must be some mirage, but now it's changed: the camera flicks back and there are cities out there. It focuses on what appear to be rectangular, dull-windowed buildings and almost minaret-ish towers or possibly lighthouses. Everything looks sandy but there's an edge before the water as though it could be St Mark's Square, the Doge's Palace and the Campanile – can we almost see contradictory cars, some people? No, it seems deserted, the camera behaves as though it doesn't understand and wobbles back to a long shot of the pouring sky, then, for reassurance, to the faces on the walls as though comparing realities. Then back again to one of the gods' islands. It's dry, there's shimmers to it like tarmac at a distance when you know it's dry, it's floating on the same water we will go to soon and look out at and see nothing at all.

But before I get there, I look back at the sugar cube of theatre because above, in an open curtained area I can't quite analyse spatially, I hear the sliding twangs and long slow notes, the sudden shill of woodwind; and I'm told 'the orchestra is warming up' – and it's that I film on my phone for forty seconds or so: no figures, just the sliding notes emerging from a building I still don't understand.

Ten Thousand Pines

At Wansongpu (Ten Thousand Pines) Writers Centre
i.m. Keith Morris

A lighter made a little moon
of Xiaodu's face, then just a star,
red as a dwarf, as though the lens
of some large telescope was jarred
as we sat drinking in the dark
and talked among ten thousand pines.

And Antony and Lian clinked
beerbottles, praised all wolves, and laughed
at endless Party toasts, gave thanks
that we'd escaped upon this raft
into a sea of needles, soft
as fish-teeth, here to gently sink.

And I thought back to floating in
the Bohai, far too west of where
it meets the Yellow Sea: that line,
that border which two waters share –
how should you know which side you were,
moonless, alone, and wholly blind?

So told them of the call I'd got
before the reading: how a friend
was walking home, how he'd been hit,
how some young driver made an end
of all his music, how all sound
had left him on that distant street.

We raised our bottles in the night
I hadn't grasped till then was full
of all the stillnesses of pine –
ten thousand bows that wouldn't lull
a jarring heart, ten thousand souls
who'd found that random borderline.

Three Lost Films

2

We were still somewhere in the temple complex and I'm not sure whether it was a Buddhist or a Daoist temple. The layout of all the temples is so similar: you enter through a porch passing between scary purple or green giants; then you're in a courtyard flanked with buildings – from the one on the left people buy massive bushels of incense, light them with some difficulty, then place them to burn in a central ash-filled stand. The inner temple building is straight ahead up a few steps where you approach the main deity past two lined-up crews of immortals or intermediaries, all life-sized at least and containing winsome women, smiling ancients and stern warriors. The God or Buddha is always flanked by two attendants and all this happens in a building with roof-timbers, columns and assorted beams painted in blue castellated patterns in shades that create recessive 3-D patterns that confuse any eye that isn't drawn to the God of the Sea or Avatar of Maternity – the one with a massive painting behind him, half-storm, half-grisaille dragon; the other attended by maidens, one of which holds a giant eyeball; all with money strewn at their feet in abundance.

Wherever we'd reached at this point in the tour, we were within box after box of temple, holiness inside holiness but somehow without growing holier – neither ourselves nor our surroundings. An equality of spirituality had been achieved, an ecumenical democracy was shared between tourist and believer, guide and temple official, priest and, in this particular courtyard, poet. Because here there was a large stand hung with every level of souvenir from pencils to costumes, from postcards to huge rubbings of the calligraphy committed to stone at this site, some of which dated back to distant dynasties. And it was a sheet of this calligraphy hanging like a peeled blackboard pelt in the shadows of the awning that had attracted Lian and Xiaodu: an inscription by Su Shi, who had stayed at the temple for a matter of days more than a thousand years before, scarcely long enough to commit these 'Notes on Reading Wu Daozi's Painting' to paper. They were remarking on how proper and perfect the hand was, almost a platonic example, until almost at the left hand edge when, suddenly, after the date, something more occurs to the poet, and he begins to write again.

They're reciting it now, almost in harmony, though Lian breaks off to explain Su Shi had almost certainly been drinking, but it's hardly necessary: the shift in their voices as they pass from the ideal to a wildness, a wilderness appended to the rational city of what was written first, is perfectly evident. I know now that what Su Shi was drinking was not the 'wine' of my translations but the *báijiŭ* of our own drinking sessions, too potent to describe as merely alcohol; and I know too that this liquor has no more changed than the characters these two poets are able to read after the night of centuries, the static frenzy of script obliterating time. But it's not this I film, but their subsequent discussion – I miss their two faces chanting: Yang Lian's long black hair wisping around his Genghis cheekbones; Tang Xiaodu's rounder features and hesitantly blinking eyes: one voice stronger and the other more melodious, its slight stammer gone, both of them lost in the text.

Yantai

The old fighter rests by the runway,
its cockpit loosened, its aerial at ease,
its fuselage a dull guttural grey.

The red star is still as bright as crayon,
lacking that mix of yellow with the dark
blood tone of Red Lantern cherries,

fetched for us from high on the tree
and eaten in the grove at Changsheung Village.
Earlier, in the Party Building, we'd eaten

without knowing those trees were set aside
for us, and put the stalks and stones
on the tables, watching Gaelic football

on the set beneath two hanging poems
that obscured the rules for Party Members:
what they might expect, what might

be expected of them. By the time
we got back on the coach, my fingers
had been stained past cherry into puce,

the colour that a flea turns blood.
And when we walked up to the reservoir
the guide had taken my hand to help me

up the rough cut causeway where
I watched the tadpoles wriggle near
the green brim. The mountains cupped us

and turned us into those dark squiggles
in the paintings, almost dissolving figures
connoting travellers, pilgrims, peasants.

Our plane takes off, conceals the MiG
behind cloud pleats. The steward hands out
the towelettes. I hesitate, then wash.

Three Lost Films

3

The third film was in Beijing when Antony and I decided to hit the hutongs one last time on the morning of our departure for the airport. We were staying in a swish low-built hotel, itself a hutong on a grand scale with rooms around two squares: the first a space where taxis could pull in, but the other a miniature garden complete with opium-boothed bar and a little massage hut where I'd been dressed in pyjamas, methodically pummelled and given medicinal tea to drink. (At lunch the day before a waiter had wielded a kettle with a spout an ell in length, always getting the tea in our tiny cups from a distance of several yards.) We turned left and left again into lanes full of bicycle repair shops, usually advertised by a single stirrup pump, and what seemed like spontaneous markets formed on wiggles in the road by two or three minivans and their sparse, fresh contents. Tight corridors between grey concrete houses were hung with washing, walls repaired with plastic, doors decorated with posters. We passed men in singlets, a boy who sat on a door-step covering his eyes, mothers slopping out buckets. We crossed a sudden busy road, a man whose T-shirt said 'Hello Boby/yesterday you are...' – and some third line we forgot immediately on plunging back into the grey labyrinth, then emerged into what seemed to be a play park by a lake.

The green area of swings, climbing-frames, and standing-stones decorated with incised characters, gave way to a walk around the lake taking in trendy new bars, boating areas (little gunboats in green with red stars on them were peddled past), a peculiar crannog of miniature houses apparently built for ducks, and another play-park where small children were pushed back and forth in swings moulded into the forms of giant goldfish. But where we first happened upon the park there was a man sleeping on the grass on a spread-out newspaper; children watching (very disparately-sized) dogs copulate; and a gathering of men gambling in tight little units around cards and mah jong sets. And in the play area, using the bars to stretch themselves, were some trim older people, perhaps in their sixties.

As we leaned on the railings by the water, we saw one of them set up a tape recorder on a picnic table, and the group resolved itself into couples, a few of them woman and woman as the old unself-consciously, silently do, in the absence of sufficient surviving males. A switch was flipped and everyone began to dance. It was a sedate, swing-based form of music, vaguely pop, vaguely oriental, and so was their dancing, full of elegant little twirls. It wasn't clear from their expressions whether they were learning or rehearsing. The music would get switched off abruptly, and – while a debate went on as to what to play next, and the tape was jammed on fast-forward or rewound in search of the start of something – the dancers would languidly practise some more, discussing and repeating their steps before embarking on another jazzy waltz about the play park. And this is what I recorded, not the moments before or after, in which we went for a bottle of cold beer on the decking of the boat club, or jumped in a rickshaw in order to dash to the hotel, catch the taxi to the airport, then lose my phone with all these films on it – none of that peace or panic, just the short whirling slow distracted moment of their dance.

Cove Park
(for Polly and Julian)

The rain would like to make us all Chinese.
I climb the hill with my umbrella fanned,
through bracken drooping like a sleeve's brocade
where hands with long quartz nails have been withdrawn.
My feet are fussy as a scholar's clogs
as I traverse the wire-suspended bridge:
two studded planks above the thickened burn
that imitates a southern love song heard
last night, and all the grasses wave the pearls
they've caught in their sharp tentacles. I stop
and look back at the loch, the dark felt hills
beyond: a centipede of mist crawls down
and, waving its antennae, starts to cross
the water, while a rainbow's banner hangs
from trees, and on Loch Long the character
for 'submarine' tears paper in its wake.

OVER THE WALL II

...to follow the complex course of descent is to maintain passing events in their proper dispersion; it is to identify the accidents, the minute deviations – or conversely, the complete reversals – the errors, the false appraisals, and the faulty calculations that gave birth to those things that continue to exist and have value for us...

FOUCAULT

What's that you say?
Speak up, I can't hear.

IAN McCULLOCH

Bothy Nichts

I take my daughter home for Easter to
that foreign country where we both began
and notice, as we look through photos from
my uncle's sixtieth in broad daylight,
the music these flashed faces shamble to
still lingers in an earthhouse in the field
behind my parents' house in Monifieth.
Long houses in the flatlands round Montrose
still hear it; it collects about Braemar
like anglers – can she smell it? Rumour of
a reel's remains, the last hangover of
a fiddle from the factor's wedding, caught
in egg-white quivering in the tea-stained shell
that still receives *Mons Graupius Broadcast Noise?*

The one-eyed legionnaire, in feeling up
that fish-wife from Auchmithie, crackles out
a half-known chorus on the doings of
a marten doon the doctor's worsted breeks.
And in the cottage where we put her cot
the door jams open on a Brownie's throat,
the floor a marmalade of carpet tiles
that we have loved and cats have pished upon;
of *Press and Journal* weddings, *Courier* snaps
that I've already scanned for old girlfriends,
the grooms afflicted by the jaundice and
each bride with an extended pubic hair
curlicued to her pow, the text transcribed
by a copious tracery of mouse-arse braille.

And everyone but her recalls this sesh,
albeit filtered through the DDT-
distended nostrils of John Laurie as
the resurrection and the requiem
become conflated in a common speak
of spiderwebs dilating up his neb.
The knife drawer skews half-open in mid-air
in a grey-grained lean-legged table that
no woman ever set or sat at once

where all the skeletons of billies sing,
cold slabs of old sliced porridge domino-
ing out, page after auto-pulping page
of still more stillborn music for the mould
accordion of these leaf-eroding hills.

Should I be glad if she can't hear it? Yet
another habbie on the habit of
the postie during coition, gumming down
twopenny blues upon the freckled small
of Janet's back? And will she bishop-curse
my shy mishandling of her bridal gift:
authentic shattered shellac scrivened with
our ersatz ceilidh code? Somehow it's passed,
all tongue- and finger-tipping into touch –
we flick away from the uncancellable
channel hotwired into the cortex, and
return our gaze to the small dog in smirr
eating up tired remains of hard-boiled eggs
we rolled away from the mouth of the tomb.

Macaroni Pie Fetish

Miss Loren is waulkin doon
thi Hilltoon in her birthday dress,
her ninepence hid ahent a macaroon
a pehcase clapped on ilka breast.

It is in tribute tae oor city
she's macaroni on her titties,
and in a greasy Wellgate caff
her fans await tae lick it aff.

Sailors Home

Between the camouflage bar, the tattoo parlour and
        the tool shop: 'Sailors Home' in brassy
        Courier Old Victorian Orphanage font
above the now-moored gate, the bewildered mail
        washed up upon its draughtboard tiles
between the arches faced with black-speckled pink marble diamonds
        meeting in the features of Poseidon blurred
        by exhaust fumes on the corner of Dock Street
and Candle Row, plants growing from its grey guttering out –
grey sandstone ship departing, showing us
its high-hipped arse of galleon, its back to the firth
        as if it set sail for the Seagate instead,
        ploughing through the toun,
        closing something in the face of memory.

At its waterline in place of anchor
        the lily and the urn of municipal Dundee,
the date as chain, 1881, and
        in place of bollards, two old sea-devil eagles
        with barnacle beards.
The pavement scarcely breaks into a wave,
        just the cracked glass tiles that let light in
        to a basement where laundry, cooking, stores
        all might have once been kept, now gone to green:
the moss a mimic of the dull dark depths they slept beside
as though they brought that heavy mistress back
and stored her in this temporary dwelling with
        its weed-dark green paintwork and
        the tropical sea-squirts, the coral letters
        of old graffiti on the Chapel door.

The cabins ascend as bleary as the weariness
        that once looked out, sinking behind their glass –
one floor filled to its dark eyelids with demarara rum;
another with the rubbery coils of oil-streaked ejaculate;
and one has a giant sucker placed to each dusty pane:
        two pale blue eyeballs fill the corner rooms –
one looking at the Custom House as though it were a language
it can no longer speak;

54

the other through
    the ghost of the Royal Arch like a pince-nez, seeking out
the Bass Rock lightship like a lobster boiled in the docks,
that sent the Ferry lifeboatmen
    to kick their slowing boots upon the bottom of the sea;
the Unicorn, whose figurine, half hippogryph half narwhal,
it can almost understand,
that mastless training ship, deck roofed over
    as though tar had been applied to stumps.

And at the soft stone rail the two men hunching in their sculpted
        oilskin hats:
    twins of the doldrums and the hollowing, troughs the size
    of whole villages they lived in once,
    calms the size and age of forests cleared for sheep,
last ambassadors from that liquid city that covers the rifts between
        the plates,
its catacombs that hold whole fleets of harvest,
mausolea of the piss-poor masses, slaves and whalers,
    serving-men and sons of the nobility of far less nations than
there are waves to cover them;
spreaders of the cold molasses mattress
that rows them in and lets them sink.

And round the broken handrail the names of admirals
whose deeds we knew or never knew as well as fingernails
    in hands that have grown shrinkles now that won't dry out
    or knew but can't remember like green glass
    too long at sea to quite see through –
names that begin to break and flake and float away:
Nelson   Cook   Blake
  Wood   Duncan
    ?Dibdin   Napier
      Hardy   Dea_
        Hall   An_ _ n

Ode to the 'New' Tay Bridge

The Storm Fiend did loudly bray,
Because ninety lives had been taken away,
On the last Sabbath day of 1879,
Which will be remember'd for a very long time.

WILLIAM McGONAGALL

Twas in the clammy autumn of 2003
I was commissioned by some madmen at the BBC
to write aboot you, rickety auld Tay railbridge
(a prospect as cheery as inhabiting a fridge),
and a turbid revelation wiz granted unto me –
disturbin fur a Scotsman afore he's hud his tea –
that William McGonagall, wha wrote aboot you furst,
wiz no a woeful poet but a thingummy far worse:
a juggernaut of doggerel, the laureate from Hell,
an icon of his era like tae Issie K. Brunel.

While Isambard build iron boats the same size as the ocean
McGonagall wrote rusty verse of abyssal proportion
devoted tae catastrophe domestic or abroad –
nae massacre or forest fire this man wad not applaud.
The fact that he wiz abstinent made me begin tae think
total calamity his substitute fur drink;
the fact that he wiz obstinant, tho brainless as a midge,
made me think aboot this Storm Fiend that he sez attacked the bridge,
for this wiz his disaster, his wee Pompeii-on-Tay:
the bridge fell doon, a haill train drooned, all on a Hogmanay...

When one surveys yir predecessor, built by Thomas Bouch,
there's an inclination to adopt a tight defensive crouch,
but it disnae tak a Storm Fiend tae plant some gelignite
like it disnae tak a genius tae pen a load o shite.
McGonagall wiz guilty, and God wiz fair but hard:
he possessed yir every atom wi the spirit of wir bard.
Each girder is a rib, and every rail a tooth,
every bolt's an eyeball, and yir redbrick piles... 'Forsooth!'
we'll hear you cry as we rattle intae toon,
'Why must they cross the River Tay while I have my troosers doon?'

NOTE: The first Tay Bridge, as McGonagall tells us, fell in 1879. Its successor was
built in 1887, and it still (touch wood) in service.

56

The Baths

The swimming-bath's blue-white barrel belly roof
extends before you for not one length but forty.
The light-globes are bright as eel-things' stingers
in black depths, and you're soon beyond the bathers,
the accidental grazing of wrist or ankle. Only
red-vested lifesavers space out the distance
standing with towels round their waists
like northern sarongs, leaning forward, staring
into the deeper and deeper water, still
perfectly clear, chlorinated, lit to the bottom,
where tiles are giving way to tesserae,
sunken floors of villas, still littered with coins
and rubber weights. Their mosaics depict
unknown deities with too many tentacles
consuming youths with glazed eyes,
the way sharks' seem lost in orgasm –
you glimpse the bitter beak amid their entrails.
And you're tiring now, the spaces between lamps
grow longer, as do the moustaches on
the occasional lifeguards – are they Victorians
or Turks, you wonder, swallowing another
involuntary mouthful, and is it brackish,
urinated? The darkness is creeping from
below you now like incontinent ink, there is
a blurry rim of sediment on all the shellfish
clustered on the pool's side. Would you cut yourself
as you got out? Would an attendant help
as your legs floundered under their own
rediscovered weight? That blaring like a whale's
grey plastic nostrils is your own breath,
every stringy stroke a tearing ended by
the spraying grunt, and your belly glows now
like the blue whale's ribs that hang above you.
You're swimming your last yards down towards
the Tay Whale's tailbone, vision greying at
the edges where you may be seeing
the wooden cubicles that lined the long-demolished
Dundee baths, each one dark, containing a

seated boy, sweating through the wetness,
his long hair tendrilling his hands; each one
the child that, as your weak slice at the waves
touches something's lip, you see you have become.

McPelvis Meddley

*I was able to trace [Elvis'] family tree, and when
it got back to Lonmay it was like striking gold.*
ALLAN MORRISON,
BBC News Online, 23.3.04

Well ye can rob his grave
for the strum o his hand
shauk the pepper frae his hips
aa ower the strand
ye can mix his voice
with-uh Jimmy Shand
but don't you
try on his blue suede kilt
yeah ye can stap aa oor lugs wi milt
but lee aff o his blue suede kilt

*

He ain't nithin but a teuchter
screwin aa the quines
pit his paw behind a pleuchter
and he's plooin thru the brine
well he got tae Carolina
but he sterted oot by swimmin Loch Fyne

*

Freh bananas
cook em thru
always use auld lard
peanut butter
he loved hoo
ye made his arteries hard

We freh Mars Bars
till they're hot,
think battered haggis brill
Elvis chose
like ony Scot
tae let his diet kill

*

He's caught in wir crap
and he cannae get oot
because we love tae roll in the gravy

Gee Memphis the sack
tell Graceland tae scoot
coz Presley's a loon and no a baby

He's rovin owre the heather
in avaricious minds
we sew gold lamé dreams
in Elvisious minds

*

He don't want tae be fae Glescae
for Glescae acts too tough
he disnae want come fae Embro
coz Embro's no a toon
worth singin of

He jist wants tae be fae Aiberdeen
leave his wallet aff the sneck
and we'll jist dip in...
oh let him be (oh let him be)
from Aiberdeen

*

Thangyew very muckle

SOFIA CITY BLUES

it
is in the dot of the i
or between the i and the t
or it's the devil knows where

but the Devil doesn't know

GEORGI GOSPODINOV
from 'Eleven Attempts at a Definition'

A Small Tune

The man honking enthusiastically on the creamy grey sac of skin in Eldon Square, the day before I left for Sofia; the man in the woolly hat who seemed to have a tune he was searching for without ever really being able to find it; the man everyone seemed to avoid, especially small dogs the same colour as the bag of skin – nonetheless seemed to have a small fortune lying in the coat spread out on the pavement before him.

It must be a small tune, to need so few notes – half a melody whistled by someone a century back as they performed a small domestic task. Not that hamstring-straining walk back up the mountain in the moonlight, back through the patchy snow, up through his breath to the farmhouse. He was silent for that, listening to the dog make difficult work of the drifts with its short legs. Not that tune full of the things he hadn't told her in the gloom of her parents' gate – he never wrote that down. But a small tune for the task of fetching a wooden cup, cracking the dull mirror of ice and dipping in the barrel, a few notes interrupted by the search to separate his face from the moon as the water settled.

I'm walking across a park in Sofia. It's lunchtime and there are dogs asleep on the grass in the March sunlight. Even the sign hanging half off a bare-branched tree looks sleepy. I'm listening to another bagpipe player who's sitting on a bench behind me and I'm looking at this huge sculpture like a gantry with tiles dropping off it, commemorating in wings and girders and cloud-gazing figures some event I can't read. It's surrounded by the most livid graffiti I can't read either, and as I walk round it, the tune on the bagpipe is drowned out by music from the cafe in the corner of the park. This music too is being piped in from somewhere else.

Rotunda of Sveti Georgi

Step down through all the fierce compacting years
into the earliest city, Serdica. It's like
getting on your knees. Get on your knees
in that sobriety of grandmas and look up –

until the thin bricks swill like noodles round
the Pantocrator's red inverted bowl,
and the fresco layers separate like cream,
each one part-revealed and part-destroyed.

Bulgarian angels stoop around its rim,
peer out among and through Byzantine saints
like men who squat to buy their brandy at
low windows in the sleety winter streets.

This is how the holy always drink –
heads mingled, immersed to their groins in feathers.

Gara Thompson

Somebody must have beat Prokopnik up
as badly as Frank Thompson and his troop
of doomed guerillas, left it face down in
the coal dust filling in its mirthless grin
of disused huts and shovellers, though the church
looked new, red-tiled beneath that tall bright ridge
of mountains showing snow through thinning birch.
We bounced across a long thin hopeful bridge
and saw the river and the railway track
entwining as they left, and then the plaque
for Gara Thompson: Communism's small
tribute upon an empty station's wall.
What did he leave? *A crossless monument*
that hoped to know the future's whole intent.

Then drove around those high containing hills:
limestone that seemed to wall in brief towns called
Sverino still, or 'beastly' in his slang,
because the Turks were ambushed there, and hanged
the rebels where they caught them; shrines where monks
found mimic etymologies for all
this rock, since Cherepishki can mean 'skull'
and 'little prick' – as was the fascist drunk
at Litakovo who was told to shoot
Frank with his weekly batches of *haidutsi*
because he was and could be seen to be a
pratenikia of solidarity.
He left a copy of Catullus, since
we cannot worship where we do not wince.

And so we drove into Lyuti Dol,
the 'hot ferocious valley' circled by all
those mountains, followed lumps of snow still lining
the road as through dropped from their truck, and then in
each village saw what seemed to be great torches
of unlit straw in metal baskets topping
telegraph poles: nests for still-absent storks
to bring good fortune back. Till then a slip
of red and white thread's worn through March, for luck

that he ran out of here, a wristbone crossed
with blood, a *martinitsa* – string you pluck
to hear how Spring's vibrating with the lost.
What did he leave? *That faith of youth*
which struggles for yet never doubts the truth.

And in another bashed-up town, the lane
that bears his name led past a breekless bairn
and up towards the unkempt bottled steps
and rambled gravel where the past is kept, a
bratska mogila by some hilltop firs,
the 'brothers' grave' for partisans who now
are held remote and nameless as dead stars,
regime fall tarnishing his martyr's crown.
And yet the silence reached that valley's shroud
of snowcaps, till we hit the Sofia road
and passed those girls who bare their bums and bras,
since what he couldn't see has come to pass.
He left a thumb-smear coin, since heads or tails
we always know Byzantium must fail.

Haidutsi: brigands, rebels; *pratenikia:* messenger, emissary.

Svetka Petka Samardzhiiska

It's night-time now in the elder frescoes
and the saints have faithfully held their poses
while darkness clusters like granular slush.

They've been torn up, scrumpled, and mostly
lost their places in the comic book
that's plastered in tatters to this strip-brick vault
by the blast of hours passing by default,
until we see their heads tilted in that gloom,
gospels for flails, their features shining
like insects
             and suddenly the entire
squat chapel is the inside of the Bible beetle.

I sit in its camphor belly and stare
at what must be the negatives of its real
markings, since its back could never be
open to those snow-plugged clouds above
Sofia, half-buried in the underpass
among the glassy shops of *boklutsi*.

Its wingcases are opening in Heaven
with all these panels fully restored:
the saints blink once in that morning
and the bug unfurls its wings,
scaled with all their naked haloes.

boklutsi: cheap souvenirs, tat.

Sofia City Blues

Eh am like thi toon whaur Eh wiz born,
meh hert is always somewhere whaur it disnae belong;
the demons of thi ages rip ma heid tae rags
and Eh cairry meh sowel in these three bags,
Eh cairry meh sowel in these three bags.

do you confuse great pop music
with being in love
well, don't apologise

Eh'm thi less travelled, unravelled man
jist a-waitin fur a slogan in thi New Bedlam
Eh'm thi man ootwith thi language, wi thi slanguage fuhl o baggage
and Eh cairry meh sowel in these three bags,
Eh cairry meh sowel in these three bags.

do you peel your mind and find
city within city within city?
don't make a career out of it

They tell me stoap translatin and enjoy thi kitsch
beginning wi thi wife o Doktor Lachnavitch
but anither ladybird jist appeared oan ma pad
she sez Eh cairry meh sowel in these three bags,
Eh cairry meh sowel in these three bags.

the bed is sandy
the bed is Sunday
the bed is bad lasagne

tissue remains

Tissue Remains

Too many hands were pressing on
my breastbone and my brow in
the great marble sandwich of the state museum.
We slid like sliced meat about the Thracian room
filled with so much gold as though
Midas had beaten up a rose garden
into this dinner service full of slurring rhyta.
The bas-relief horsemen insisted
on cornering their boars with always
one hand flung out behind them
not clutching a spear but letting the reins stream
through their casually tugging long fingers
which would only take a millennium
to rearrange themselves into
the next door icons' serpentine blessing machines
of still more hands. But for now
all the faces were Alexander clones
so that was never where my eyes could rest
till the skull-bulb helmets drew us,
their tight-lipped spaces that hold
exact absences, to the case in which
earth-coloured armour propped on perspex shoulders
and shinbones. And the greaves,
that word that's almost a wound,
had their own card that told us
what survives the centuries' ceaseless fingers
is less than the step I couldn't take away:
'Bronze, traces of leather straps, tissue remains.'

rhyta (plural): drinking cups.

The Bear
(for Fadia & Mark)

We're not long out of the blue bare dome
of the Banya Bashi mosque, empty except
for some bloke from Luton, when
we meet the bear. Everything had seemed
so familiar till the look on its face.

The Roma on the other end of the chain
plays that little fiddle that stares you down
like the Cretan lyre, and the great bear lifts
one paw as though to rest it on the skull
of one of these someones constantly

passing, each far more naked in
their negligent gaze as one foot shifts
to the beat, and I find I'm staring at
the jaunty red scarf instead of the strap
around its jaws. This bear has

another pattern to obey,
the way the painters in Boyana did,
abandoning the Byzantine style
to fill the barrel of the chapel's chest
with a crusting flood of cruelties:

how this flank is skewered by a painted spear
but that eye's removed by an actual chisel;
the feast of radishes, garlic and defacements
arranged according to local harmonics
that must mean the lovely flaking Desislava,

the doomed Sebastocrator Kaloyan,
stare at me from the bear's matt eyeholes,
the whole Second Kingdom is jostled in there
between the Tatars and the Turks.
Clearly the bear is jerking at the end

of the same Ottoman rope as Vassil Levski,
its paw raised in that saluting fist
Frank Thompson lifted before Stoyanov's
firing squad – and then, before I get on
to the communists and their umbrellas,

the fit is past, the bear is back on all fours,
all the fizz of history drains from my brain,
and I can see from its attitude that it
hasn't taken a step: the entire *horo* took place
within the singular emptiness that is

my angry skull. So the bear exits, pursued
by me and the Roma and the bearded boy
from Luton and we four sit awhile
in the old mosque reciting prayers
in a further language none of us knows at all.

RABOTNIK FERGUSSON

Can you nae ither theme divine
To blaw upon, but my engyne?

ROBERT FERGUSSON

Ya tvoi sluga
Ya tvoi rabotnik

KRAFTWERK
The Robots

Rabotnik Fergusson

1

When Fergusson awoke in Hell
or mebbe Heaven – wha can tell?
he noticed (eftir this weird smell,
    some kinna plastic,
no that he kent thi stuff himsel)
    he felt fantastic!

Undeemis, since thi final oor
that he could mind afore thi smoor
o daith, he'd tynit ilka pooer
    o rational thocht
and yammert waur nor ony cooard
    and wiz fairfocht.

Thi gashed pow, bootit lyk a baa
beh'iz stairs, that he hud happt in straa –
uts wound jist wiznae there at aa,
    insteid, a dome
nae mair his own nor a doo's a craw
    (a hardent foam).

He upped and gowped aroond thi Pit,
a michty well aa clagged wi glit
in which grecht mowdiehills did sit
    lyk midden moonds,
geean aff nae guff o shit,
    but muttrin soonds.

Thi furst o these he geed a lookie
and frae uts midst stuck a bahookie
uts cheeks aa prentit lyk a bookie
    wi wurds he kent.
The doup crehd out then, 'Nae mair nookie!
    Eh've peyed meh rent.'

Undeemis: unusual; *smoor:* smothering; *tynit:* lost; *ilka:* each; *yammert:* jabbered;
fairfocht: exhausted; *pow:* forehead; *happt:* wrapped; *doo:* dove; *gowped:* gaped;
clagged: besmirched; *glit:* filth; *mowdiehills:* molehills; *guff:* stench; *bahookie,*
doup: backside.

'Is that thi behind of auld Blind Harry?'
'Wha'd no be blind this deep in slurry?'
'Whit's happened here? Tell me yir story.
        First in oor verse,
you shid be thronit in yir glory...'
        'Wi a cushioned erse!'

'Meh fate's thi semm as mony here
mooled in auld words year oan year.'
Here Fergusson drabbilt in thi dross
and foond ut wiz aa 'ȝ's and 'Quho's.
'Thi Sea of Letters rains ode-banes
and deein habbies till meh fame
is jeeled aneath thi jaain deid
an naewan's left wi nous tae read
meh tale o hoo the Waallace focht
tae find the jesp whaur tyrants wrocht
a gag and blindfold fur meh land,
but nane's noo left tae undirstand –
the pressure oan meh mou and ehs
is sic, nae glints fae meh wurds rehz.
But lehbry-drones they still descend
and stap meh epic up meh end –
they meisure up meh maisterstick
and syne they yaise ut fur a dick.
Nae love's intendit beh this thrust
fur whit dae robots ken o lust?'

'Whit deils are these tae torment you
and fyle yir anus fur a flue?
(This 'robots' wurd is faur too new –
        ut maks me fyke.)'
'No hauf as much as being used
        tae park thir bike.'

'We're at thi future's mercy here
and graithit in thi future's gear;
and in this place o un-free men
we deal in wurds we dinnae ken.

mooled: buried; *deein:* dying; *jeeled:* coagulated; *jesp:* gap, loophole; *mou:* mouth; *ehs:* eyes; *lehbry:* library; *stap:* ram; *maisterstick:* piece of work produced by a craftsman to prove himself qualified; *fyke:* fidget or itch; *graithit:* equipped.

As you ascend this hellish shaft
ye'll mebbe find a wiser chaft
tae explicate. But hear meh verse
afore ye laive; let me rehearse
a sang that micht alleviate
these paiks Eh get fur bein late.'

ODE TO FREEDOM

'Fredome is ane nobill thing',
it chaps the heids aff safty kings;
fredome gets breathed in by Scots
like helium by aquanauts.

Fowk pass free hoors on the Broo
like polar bears dae in the Zoo;
auld hippies shag their best freend's lass
then gae hame on their free bus pass.

Fredome is the cure for stress,
it taks the crease oot o Sta-Prest;
it taks the metre oot o verse,
lets things hing oot that wance were terse.

Scots are free tae write like this,
thir readers free tae tak the piss;
we're free-er when we scrieve in Lallans,
English jist restricts oor talents.

Tak awa oor audience,
tak awa oor common sense:
the thing ye cannae kerry oot's
oor fredome tae shoot at wir ain big foot.

Fredome's whit they gee tae schmos
wha hae nae ither place tae go:
Scots Language rulebooks, squatters' richts –
last wan free kick oot thi lichts.

chaft: jaw; *paiks:* blows; *safty:* weakling; *Broo:* the Dole; *scrieve:* write.

2

A guid Scots mile across an deep's
thi dungeon whaur thi auld bards sleep
and Fergusson sclimmed unca heaps
    afore he raxed
thi sides that streik up sterk and steep –
    syne he relaxed:

therr wiz a spiral gyrin path
aboot as thick as ae roof lath
that woond up lyk his eme's black wrath
    intae thi vapour
tae coont thi coils wad foil the math
    o baney Napier.

Sae up he trauchlet – why remain
oan thon sea-flair o sunken fame?
but as he rose an oorich strain
    attacked his lugs,
a bizzin and bizarre refrain
    that hoatched lyk bugs.

And aa thi air wiz thick wi wurds
that spooled and swooped and sang lyk burds
and swaarmed lyk flehs upon thae curds,
    his curlin herr,
and in his mooth they shoved and shirred
    till in despair

he spat oot, 'Wha's auld tunes ur these
that heat thi daurk lyk a disease
and hop upon me waur nor fleas?'
    and heard a groan;
then said a figure oan uts knees,
    'Eh am Anon.'

'And fur these seeven turns o steps
aboot the channerin well
ye're passin whaur thi ballads ur kept
and soond is sicht and smell.

unca: unusual; *raxed:* reached; *syne:* then, next; *lath:* tile; *eme:* uncle; *trauchlet:*
laboured wearily; *oorich:* unearthly; *hoatched:* swarmed; *shirred:* shifted like wheat
in a breeze; *waur:* worse; *channerin:* grumbling, gravelly.

'And aa aroond thi charnel reek
o deid sangs maun be sniffed,
and in thi waas thi nemmless jaas
aa champ within thir shifts.'

And here thi figure stood and drew
a curtain back lyk silk
that wiz a strand o language and
ahent ut, lyk a whelk,

therr wiz a roond wee door o horn
ajar tae show a space:
'Here's whaur Eh lig until self-scorn
commands me oot tae pace.'

'Eh thocht,' said Fergusson, 'Eh saw
ye kneel as though in prayer.'
'Meh lugs ur raw whaur clegs aa gnaw:
sall we ascend thi stair?'

And as they climbed, 'Ye're no confined?'
he asked his shroodit maik.
'Some licht that's leachin fae yir mind
compels me in yir wake.'

Sae Fergusson looked at thi groond
and through thi mirky air
and saw ut daurkened whaur he frooned
(which garred him froon thi mair).

And as they climbed thi clamour fell
as tho a pley began
or some stern judgement. Fur a spell
they clambirt, fit owre hand,
in pechs and silence till they cemm
oantae a braider ledge
oan whilk a stack o buiks cast flemms
sae they cuid tak a gledge
        thru empty nicht

lig: lie; *lugs:* ears; *clegs:* horseflies; *maik:* partner; *garred:* made; *pechs:* pants;
gledge: sharp glance.

tae whaur lyk hoolet's een twa mair
sma flares werr burnin bricht,
syne his companion's upwird stare
revealed an ugsome sicht:
tapsalteerie oan an X
a man wiz crucifehd;
against thi stang he trehd tae flex
his heid, and failed, and sedd:
      'This damnit licht –

'Eh canna tell gin you are drones
or makars lyk tae me –
nae maitter noo, come brak ma bones:
Eh'll naither dee nor dree.'
'Eh think this cheil's some kinna bard,'
the shroodit man replehd.
'While Eh'm lyk you, sae scoored and scaured,
Eh ainly ken Eh've dehd
      and roam this nicht.'

'Whit is yir nemm, and why dae these
buiks blacken thon braw pow?'
asked Fergusson, 'and brither, please,
whit means thae ither lowes?'
'Eh yaised tae be crehd Henryson,
and hing here fur thi sin
o verse that isnae Anglophone,
as dae baith him and him
      thru endless nicht.

And as they gandered owre thi gap
they saw them: furst thi torch
and then thi cross, syne owre thi drap,
thi heids thir ain wark scorched.
'Thi wan is Gavin Douglas, wha
translatit Virgil furst,
thi tither is ma fere Dunbar,
and baith o them ur curst
      tae hing in nicht.

hoolet's een: owl's eyes; *ugsome:* ugly; *tapsalteerie:* head over heels; *stang:*
wooden bar; *dree:* endure; *chiel:* man; *lowes:* burns; *fere:* brother, companion.

'Thir crime's committin aa thir craft
intae condampit leid
lyk crammin gowd intae thi chaft
o wan aareddy deid.'
Fur aa this speech pair Fergusson
hud stuck therr lyk a rock:
thae nemms hud geed his hert three stouns
and garred his tongue tae lock
     an steek that nicht.

'Maister,' at last, 'Eh ken sae well
beh wurd alane – tho tae yirsel
Eh see that this is truly Hell –
     that we shid meet
maks here and Heiven cruelly mell,
     baith wersh and sweet.'

'Eh dinna ken this stanza, but
Eh hear ut fit ye, shoe tae fuit,
and in this drouth Eh feel yir glut
     o faith spill oot;
thi woond ye cairry's lyk tae split
     ye, roof tae root.

'Be shair that faith's in wurds, no men
wha anely care tae mak wurds bend
and hear nae means but anely ends –
     and fear thae sharks
wha snifter oot yir sowel's ain scent;
     and this tale mark:'

THE PARLIAMENT OF FLIES

Since thi Bruce abruptly left
Dame Spider's duin baith warp an weft;
she's turned a cave intil a hoose
whaur ilka windie is a noose,
and oan her plate thi flehs debate
thi heritage that she relates:

condampit: condemned, damaged; *leid:* language; *stouns:* blows; *mell:* mingle;
wersh: bitter; *drouth:* thirst.

fae MacBeth and his guid wumman
and fae Balliol tae Comyn,
fae the Waallace tae thi Bruce
        (wha'd jaloose whit they'd let loose?)
        thi line o Scotia's written doon
        in dreebles fae a drehd auld spune.

And in that hame she catches gowd
and haps ut in a paper shroud
and sooks aa value fae a nation
tae construct hir fleecin-station
and aa thi flehs hing in her wab
and ask if this riff cemm fae Rab:
fae thi regents and thi kings
that niver kent or learnt a thing,
and fae Darnley tae Dundas
wha led us up Dunnottar Pass,
        thi screed of Alba's scrievat oot
        in sealice oan a fousty troot.

And when her parliament o flehs
allot thirsels a wee pay-rehz
they find her fangs ur in therr wame
and creh oot 'Chaps, let's stoap thi gemm,'
and as she eats them erse tae ee
she hums this air wi muckle glee:
fae MacDiarmid tae MacLean
(wha's oor communistic thane?)
and fae Dewar tae McConnell
and fae Margo tae MacDonald
        thi sang o Scotland gangs lyk this:
        whit ye cannae buy will aye be missed.

3

'Ut's time noo, cwa, tae speel thi waa
lyk guid Scots sots oan usquebaa
afore thi Sifters stert tae faa,'
        spake up Anon.
'We're no oan oor richt shelves ava.
        Wheesht: therr's a drone!'

screed: writing; *chaps:* expression calling a truce; *speel:* climb.

And in thi midst o mist an stoor
a thing, pairt-pencil and pairt-flooer,
wiz hingin in a thrum o pooer
        and fykin roon,
pairt-hummin bird, pairt-fishin lure,
        alert fur soond.

'Ahent thi bonfire o meh buiks,'
thi makar whispert, 'ere ut looks –
yir pow's licht's lyk a bealin plook
        oan the neb o a hure.'
Meanwhile Anon stepped oan the stook
        that bleezed sae pure.

The flemms devoored his hempen shrood
and shot sae heich and cracked sae lood
till Henryson's big taes begood
        tae loss thir herr:
thi drone ascendit in thon clood
        as on a chair.

Thi boady that hud been sae burnt
stepped fae thon pyre sae peeled he'd turnt
intil a kinna waulkin current
        o quills and ink.
'Cwa speel,' it spoke, 'since we have earnt
        a space tae think.'

A weary *vale*, syne aince mair
thi lang upgangan, stair beh stair,
as stith as Clydesdales driven up
a stegh brae beh thi cleeshin whup.
And ony heat thi deeps hud helt
wiz skinned aff lyk this cratur's pelt.
Ut strode aside him tho uts feet
werr clackin nibs, and geed aff gleets
lyk brizzes in thi breeze, and reeked
o rubber and thi ile that's streaked
through cauld sand in an Angus haar.

---

stoor: dust; *thrum:* vibrate; *bealin plook:* festering pimple; *stook:* a shock of cut
sheaves; *bleezed:* blazed; *begood:* began; *cwa:* come away; *upgangan:* rising; *stith:*
severe; *stegh:* steep; *cleeshin:* lashing; *gleets:* glints; *haar:* sea-mist.

Ut didnae talk nor did he daur
until he vizzied up abune
a sicht sae orra ut wad stoun
a stirk and spur a mule tae speech:
thi pit's raw rim wiz in thir reach.

Ut foarmed tae his up-anglet sicht
an oon egg oval filled wi licht
diffusely, lyk thi sun thru fog,
and raggit lyk a reugh-saaed log;
and luked sae like a liddit ee
he laughed, 'Eh've seen worse wink at me!
And whit ur aa thae lash-lyk things
that kick and kelter roond uts ring?'
'They are the legs o danglin men
wha grup thi grit wi piton-pens,'
thi black electric voice of his
aquyntance, quiet as thi hiss
o coal gas, filled his ears. 'They fear
thi faa Eh noo suspeck that we're
recovrin fae, intil a dark
sae fell that you forget yir wark
or nemm – that mine's wiz Wedderburn
Eh'm nearly shair. Eh've still tae learn
whit maks you cast this moidert gloam –
we'll update in thi uppir dome.'

'A Wedderburn? A patriot!'
'Up here we're neither men nor Scots.'

'Which brither ur ye?' 'Dinna ken.'
'At least we baith cuid wield a pen.'

'*Complaynt* or *Godly Ballates* or
thi plays noo tint upon thon floor –

thi reason Eh am oan this vaige
is nae man noo wull read a page –

---

vizzied: saw; *abune:* above; *orra:* odd; *stirk:* young bullock, gelding; *oon egg:* egg
laid without a shell; *reugh-saaed:* roughly sawed; *kelter:* struggle; *moidert gloam:*
dazed look; *tint:* lost; *vaige:* voyage.

and that is why thi drones torment,
and that is why Eh think ye're sent.'

'Whit can Eh dae?' 'Ye mak us scrieve –
oor pangs ur fur that span relieved.'

'Aye, scribble skits sae negative
nae wunner Scots sae barely lives.'

Beh noo they'd raxed thi lip utsel
whaur bardies dandlet, pissed an telt,
shat and tattlet, kissed an fell
        intae thi void –
thir reputation, missed an knelled,
        thir voice destroyed.

And Fergusson, wha wiz annoyed
tae hear hoo he shid be employed,
haaled ane back ower fae thi side
        and asked his nemm.
'Eh am Mark Alexander Boyd,
        and whit's your gemm?'

'Wan perfick sonnet – sing wan mair!'
'Eh think ye dinna ken hoo rare
sic things micht be, but see meh fere
        Montgomery:
He wiz thi author o some quair –
        Cherrie and Slae.'

Boyd then hung himsel back ower
thi pit and geed up sic a glower
at wan wha wad extend his hour
        o matchless fame,
that Fergie thocht, 'This feckless shower
        Eh'll stamp tae shame.'

Montgomery raised a cautious finger,
'Ye're seekin oot some antique singer,
yet you're nae Sifter, torment-bringer
        tae thae wha fail
tae modernise and wish tae linger
        ayont thi pale

lyk meh pal Boyd. Perhaps ye feel
thi sang utsel is aa that's real
and maks thi readers' needs aa heal
    and laives nae scar –
but we hae nane, and hence thi steel
    and syne thi tar.'

And here he wagged in Fergie's face
a leg stump wi a cicatrice
o script upon ut. 'Gin yir Grace
    wad care tae hear,
this type o portrait micht suffice
    fur nexteryear:'

THE WEE YANG

They pit thi Wee Yang tae thi Test
that sorts oot which Scots ur thi best –
    and foond he couldnae sing:
he'd stert wan verse, furget thi rest;
and he widna wear his stringy vest,
    and his oxters didnae ming.
He left thi hohos til his brither,
    thon big bahookie Billy;
he left thi drinkin til his mither
    and didnae flash his willy.
        They'd invite him tae write things
          aboot thi wurkin class,
        and keep it grim, they'd peep at him,
          or else you shall not pass.

He didnae gae ti thi clubs they'd listed,
or pley up links wi thi mony-mistit
    Pissheids o the Isles;
thi Wee Yang wiznae that quick-fistit;
ye kicked a baa at him he missed it –
    and sae he flunked thir Trials.
He tramped nae machairs, nor climmed Monroes,
    he niver sailed a yaat;
he fucked nae Farquhars, wrote nae prose,

ming: stink.

pleyed pipes or strangilt cats –
    but this hero of a zero,
        whas soul wiz oan thi dole,
    he had not got plans for Some Like It Hotland
    sae kept oot that own goal.

Thi Jockstar Test thi Wee Yang failed
huz left oor culture sair impaled
        upon St Andrae's Cross;
thi types of Scot wi which we're nailed
are: London Licklips, Kilt n Kailed,
        and Buckies actin Boss –
that's anely three, fur hingin free,
    tho mebbe no fur lang,
's a pen in a haund that still can dree
    belangs tae thon Wee Yang.
        There's roisters and oysters
           and shysters fuhl o stink:
        North Britain gets written
           wi pearlies in uts ink.

4

They left him beh thon canyon's edge
and waulked oan thru a brittle sedge
o type that like a smutty *neige*
        kept rainin doon
fae bead-shapet cloods. 'Well, we're but fledged
        and gaun tae groond,'

said Fergusson, and scanned this lift
whaur abacus-like cloods wad shift
and thru thi bories and thi rifts
        he saw drones flock.
Said Wedderburn, 'We're gien a gift
        we maun unlock.

'A stanza is like solid air:
Eh scance that this ane wull compare
        wi sonnets and thir like
and serve us as funicular –

bories: gaps in clouds; *scance:* scan, look critically at.

85

a room that views, a bird-brain car –
        tae save us baith a hike.
wi that his shape seemed tae unsneck
        as tho ut coiled uts micht
ut oped uts mou and gan tae shauk
        an spued oot cauld blue licht,
                morphosin in throes un-
                        till it wiz inside out:
                unfettert, pure letters,
                        his inner stanza's shout

wiz, 'Here Eh am, baith vehicle
and vaiger, skeleton and skill
        tae muve ye: tak a ride,
let verse utsel transport ye til
Parnassus's ain windiesill
        and even luke ootside.'
And oan thi shouders o thon stave
        he rode intae a cirque
of air that wisnae skeh, a nave
        that niver kent a kirk:
                aa roon them thi soond cemm
                        when cabinets snick shut,
                a flickerin and snickerin,
                        a speed-read o low wut.

Wance thru thi cloods thi click and throb
wiz clearly drones that did thir job
        within thi upper air,
and aa within a whummlin globe
uts waas aa combs thae robots probed
        and each contained a quair.
They hid ahent a shuttle-clood
        and foond ut tae wiz text
as tho ye strippt a lehbry nude
        and left thi wurds perplexed.
                Through columns o volumes
                        they neared thon ooter waa
                sae slowly, though, beh folio,
                        fur fear that they wad faa.

ABOVE: *unsneck:* unlock; *whummlin:* tumbling; *quair:* volume.
OPPOSITE: *dwaums:* dreams.

86

Fur in thae dwaums in which ye fleh
confidence keeps ye in thi skeh
      and theirs wiz rinnin low:
whit if this metre's motor dehd
or they werr seen? They prophesehd
      disaster, sank and slowed.
and grabbed beh luck a haundle wrocht
    fae ehvry, and a door,
and draigged a draaer until ut caucht
    a mile abune thi floor.
        And ramblet an scramblet
          till they were in that box;
          and yelled 'Heh?' repelled beh
          uts contents' creh, 'Nae knocks?'

Ut seemed tae be a coffin but
as big as some auld shepherd's hut.
Uts owner chortlet at his wit
      although attached
tae a fiddle strung fae his ain gut,
      'See whit Eh've hatched?'

He lauched and pleyed a hennie jig,
'Deil tak thae drones, dye hae a fig
Eh could refuse tae gee thum? Whig
      or Tory, sir?
Let's hae a gless o Cameron Brig
      and stories, rare!'

Thi stanza noo hud self-invertit
and wiz tae Wedderburn revertit
wha beh this man wiz sae divertit
      he said, 'Eh'll go!
and till this tiltin room's desertit
      tell whit Eh know:'

SONG OF THE KETTLE-BOILER

Ilka wee boy that is boarn in Dundee
learns hoo tae fail fae the age o three
fur while his ma's aff rinnin STV
he waatches his da trehin tae mak up thi tea
he's a biler, kettle-biler

87

Ilka young laddie that gangs tae thi gemm
sees thi Dees or thi Ayrabs baith actin as lame
fur shite and manure wull aye smell thi semm
lyk thon rose that they creh beh sum ither nemm
rosa biler, kettle-biler

In thi deys when thi men wid rin aff tae catch whales
they hid ahent blubber, in bergs and up sails
till an Inuit wifie jist pops up and yells
'Eh've Franklin's auld kettle, come bile ut yersels!
Coz ye're bilers, kettle-bilers.'

Sae ilka young man when he's laivin thi skail
fur thi dole or thi college is shair he wull fail
thi meenit the rector is sayin, 'Guid luck,'
is thi meenut he kens that he's totally fucked –
he's a biler, kettle-biler

'Anither chant that puhls thi chain
and sends aa hope tae choke thi drain.
Furgive me, but that's no thi strain
　　　thi Hegh taucht me!'
'Mair fowk wi owre much oan thir brain –
　　　and fae Dundee!'

'Auld Reekie's whaur Eh truly wrote
and Allan Ramsay cut meh coat.'
'Ye're near meh era. Ramsay? – not
　　　thi younger Rab?
Precentor o thi habbie, throat
　　　untimely nabbed?'

'Eh wiznae shair gin ut wiz you
or wha,' said Wedderburn, 'tho thru
thi Archive aa yir warks are strewn
　　　beh Sifters, Eh
wad piece them back till guid as new
　　　they kissed meh eh.'

ABOVE: *Dees, Ayrabs:* Dundee and Dundee United FCs; *the Hegh:* the High School,
Dundee; *precentor:* an official appointed by the Kirk Session to lead the singing
by singing the line for the congregation to repeat.
OPPOSITE: *drobbed:* pricked with a sharp instrument; *splore:* exploit.

'You dae that tae?' thi fiddler asked.
'Ut helps thi centuries tae pass.'
'Eh steek them in meh whisky cask
        syne that's lang dreh.'
'This stanza's like a secret flask
        and that's nae leh.'

'They didnae huv it in meh dey
sae tell me hoo ut cemm tae pley
that Scottish note perfervidly
        since in these times
thi drones huv drobbed us till, at bay,
        we fear tae rhyme.'

A HABBIE HISTORY

Here comes the bauld stanzaic lore
that maks aa modernistics snore:
a man caad Sempill fur a splore
        wrote 'Habbie Simson',
a piper's elegy – and more:
        oor bards saw crimson.

(That's bagpipes, by the wailin way –
whit is a fiddler loon tae say?)
It's hauf-lament and hauf in play
        that gees the twist:
a fact that in his morbid lay
        auld Wordsworth missed.

But Allan Ramsay and young Rab
that's listin here jist hud tae grab
it fur the Scots Revival. Rab
        (that's Burns – keep up!)
wha paid fur this pair boy's grave slab
        wiz jist a pup.

'The Daft Days', 'Caller Oysters', 'To
the Tron-Kirk Bell' showed whit tae do:
Burns took the habbie till a new
        heicht wi the likes
o his addresses tae a crew
        o subtle tykes.

89

The Deil, a moose, a daisy, drink;
the haggis (damn whit veggies think!);
there's Death and Dr Hornbook's jinks
    and Holy Willie;
a louse, his mare, his mates, mair drink,
    and bein silly.

It maks ye rax for far mair rhymes
at a faster pace than the sad hauf-mimes
o normal formal verse: its chimes
    can syncopate;
it's bagpipe ragtime, bop's sublime
    Scots drinkin mate.

The habbie sometimes taks Burns' name
because ut's apt fur Burns-like games
but, billies, ut wad be a shame
    if that wiz aa:
the fitbaa needs nae player's fame,
    sae pass the baa!

5

This sang's effect oan Wedderburn
wiz mair undeemis tae discern
than ony earlier: thi pirn
        oan whilk wiz spooled
that tolter speerit spun an girned
        fae croon tae gool.

his attomy o pulsin ink
spilled oot in cuttlefishy jinks
then lyk a kraken aa did sink
        till wi a moan
a cylinder hung therr, mim, perjink –
        a thrummin drone,

and in a voice wi nae inflection:
'unit detecting file infection/
quarantine in pictish section' –
        a licht lyk bane
spreid frae uts heid in ilk direction
        till aa wiz gane.

A LULLABY WHILE RESETTING

In ablow thi bedfu
glows a headfu o
drunken clunkertonies' banes
and brabblachan, ma jo:
nicher-nickle-naethin
gets thi loon his links
sae lift thi lid oan ae thing
a lad o pairties thinks.

Shine MacFarlane's bouet
aboot a farlan's loot
o sunken leesum lillilus
and fallachans o doot:
tirlie-tocher-totum
gies thi gilly's go,
sae heeze me oan thi hodrum
a lad o pairties knows.

When Fergusson awoke in Heiven
or mebbe Hell, fur wha'd believe in
a place whaur guid fowk rise lyk leaven
    intae thi lift?
His furst thocht wiz, 'Aa thon wiz reevin,
    and noo Eh'll drift.'

He ligged upon a cot o verse –
wan aakwirt rhyme stuck in his arse
but itherwise nocht did exerce
    his weary harns,
sae rowled and saa thi universe:
    aa eager starns.

OPPOSITE: *billies:* brother, fellow member of a craft; *pirn:* spool; *tolter:* unsteady; *girned:* complained; *gool:* groin; *attomy:* body; *mim, perjink:* neat, precise.
ABOVE: *clunkertonies:* jellyfish; *brabblachan:* something small or worthless; *ma jo:* my dear; *nicher-nickle-naethin:* composite of snicker and the term represented by the letter N on a totum, or four-sided top; *Macfarlane's bouet:* the moon, *fig.* a reiver's lantern; *farlan:* a long box into which herring are emptied for gutting; *leesum lillilus:* lovely lullabies; *fallachans:* hoarded materials; *tirlie-tocher-totum:* composite of a whirling top with an endowment; *heeze:* hoist; *hodrum:* imitative expression for traditional Scottish music; *lift:* sky; *reevin:* raving; *exerce:* perform; *harns:* brains; *starns:* stars.

91

'Eh sedd we'd rax thi windiesill
and hae a hing and mebbe yell
at aa thi planets passin till
        thi truth appeared,'
thi drone sedd beh his side, 'Be still,
        and not afeared.

'Eh wiz thi parrymauk o thon
pair makar, made tae guide ye oan
yir purgin vaige fae zone tae zone
        and also test
which o thi prisoners' latest poems
        wad be thi best.'

'Is this anither torture?' 'No,
Eh mean tae let aa lilters go.
Thi lithert that in clinkers row
        Eh cannae help.
But which is which Eh wadna know
        withoot your skelp.

'Maist sing within thir programmes: you've
become a Trojan, wan that muves
them fae thir damned familiar grooves –
        Eh heard some seeds,
but Hogg rekindlet wholly pruves
        you dae thi deed.'

'Hogg?' 'He's thi fiddler Eh've jist sent
doon tae thi pit whaur you werr pent
whaur he will mebbe circumvent
        baith drap and drones
and force his feres tae reinvent
        thir art fae groans.

He pulled anither curtain back
of wurds that naewan yaised –
*dirry danton, maundrel, swack,
forspeak, gundy, hivie, paise* –
and Fergusson luked doon, amazed.

---

parrymauk: double; *maker:* poet; *lithert:* lethargic; *clinkers:* broken rocks; *row:* roll; *skelp:* smack; *dirry danton:* dance, intercourse; *maundrel:* idle tale; *swack:* sudden blow; *forspeak:* bewitch; *gundy:* toffee; *hivie:* wealthy; *paise:* weigh up.

'Behold the Biblioglobe, whaur text
is gloyed tae mak thi makars wha
wance babblet ut: they're fleeshed and sexed
and syne assesst whaur each maun faa
dependin gin they're read at aa.'

And aa thi leid that breenged abreid
wiz here and therr coagulatit
beh draves o drones intil a heid
or haund, and aa these werr collatit
till anither bardie wiz creatit.

He saw three mair wi ootspreid airms
begin thir slaw descent thru nocht
still trailin oot thir silky thairms
whaur dozent robots trehd tae wrocht
an innard fae an inward thocht.

'Why dae they punish us sae cruelly?'
'Whit dae ye think a drone is but
some files that cannae sing? They thirl
yir breist because they cannae hut
thi seat o aa yir foarmir wit;

'and hae nae standirts fur thir rage
but rank utility – thi likes
o me's a misprint oan wan page
o thir vast manual. As fur tykes
lyk you? As strange as rumplefykes

'fur wan withoot an anus.' 'Hence
thir focus oan wir nether pairts?'
'That wiz ablow, up here it's sense
that aye defeats them; in these pairts –
well, look upon these robots' Laird...'

A throne made frae thi skellington
o a sperm whale wi uts evry bone
scrimshawed wi script, and oan ut one

gloyed: hastily threshed; breenged: rushed; thirl: pierce; rumplefykes: itchy anuses.

whas heid wiz crooned wi girders rigged
intae a shauchlin roond o brig
complete wi train tae spleet his wig,

and aa supportit oan thi backs
o willin drones wha queued in stacks
tae ride upon that puffer's tracks.

And as they reeled aroond thi rails
thae robots sortit oot thi mail
and thir cry wiz aye, 'Anither sale!'

And in that din thi trippin fiss
o that sad king luked oot o place
as he received thir ranty praise:

his cheek wiz haddock crossed wi vellum
and tho they scored his cerebellum
he still hud rhymes he hud tae tell um.

'Whit's thon metre? Whit's yon yarn?
He's garglet in thi Dichty Burn!'
'Thi Grecht McGonagall, ye'll learn,

'huz naither knack nor need fur feet:
thi universe adores his leets,
and him alane frae here they read.'

Fergusson turned, looked oot thi gless,
'Sae oot there's really emptiness,
and in here Hell withoot redress.'

'Ye'd raither nae verse e'er wiz set
nor ane o his?' 'He's jist thir pet,
pair drauntin dowfart drooned in sweat.

'But wance mair tae thi parapet —'
he yelled doon, 'Gee us silence yet!'

ABOVE: *shauchlin:* unsteady, down at heel; *ranty:* boisterous; *leets:* list.
OPPOSITE: *toomness:* emptiness; *frawart:* contrary; *swarrach:* swarm; *ae:* one.

6

'Ye'll hae that sune eneuch, Eh fear
noo that they ken we baith ur here.'
'Sae that's me oot upon meh ear?'
    'Worse, Eh expect –
an ear lyk yours is subtle gear
    they wad dissect.

'Eh'd better set ye free.' 'Tae pace
thru aa thon toomness?' 'Ooter space?
No quite. We're in that ither place
    you caa thi mune:
exile tae uts dusty face
    is meh last boon.'

And as a frawart swarrach flockit
they slid intae a kind o socket
atween inside and oot, and lockit
    uts glessy door.
'Eh doot but that's meh pension dockit,
    still, ae wurd more:

'afore Eh let ye oot ye should
ken hoo this system wiz begood –
we've meenuts till thon mislearnt crood
    cut thru thi gless;
relax, and oan thi cosmos brood,
    syne aa things pass.

'Since Wedderburn wance wrote aboot
thi stars, ut's apt that Eh pint oot
that ilka planet huz been put
    tae better use
than huddin rocks – tho Man did scoot
    tae Betelgeuse

'langsyne, he left his lehbries here
fur robots tae administer...'
'They're nearly thru, and tho Eh'm sweir
    tae interrupt...'
'...or hear thi index o thi spheres?
    Eh'll keep ut cluppt.'

SONG OF THE INDEX OF THE SPHERES

'The Yirth is Yankish literature
and that includes thi Brits,
but anely those wh'are Anglopure –
thi mune's fur aa us shits.

'The Scandies and Italians split
wee Mercury in hauf
since pairt is frosnit, pairt is lit
(tae say which is a gaffe).

'The French Academy's on Venus,
naturellement,
tho De Sade nae langer huz a penis
Bardot's furiver blonde

'Thi German bunkirs sunk in Mars
while thru uts deserts roamed
thi Spanish Rozinante-cars
nor foond thir pleisure-dome.

'Thi asteroids were best employed
by Jews and Ayrabs – juist
aboot agreed that these indeed
werr Jerusalem, concussed.'

'Sae which wey noo is Mecca or
dae books no huvtae pray?'
'Fehv Babylons huv been explored,
but mair Eh couldna say.

'That Jupiter wiz Russian sent
the US in a strop
sae Turgenev and aa werr meant
tae bide i thi Big Red Spot.

'Pa Saturn wiz auld Chinee's hame,
thon foonder o thi Wey,
uts rings tae poems rearranged
maist calligraphically.

ABOVE: *frosnit:* frozen. OPPOSITE: *primely:* well-packed; *coupt:* knocked over.

'In Neptune's depths thi coral lore
o thon Subcontinent
that furst perceived thi Void wiz stored,
and uts munes werr primely Zenned.

'Uranus wiz whaur Africa
supposedly wad bide,
but funds werr rinnin short, *hélas* –
nane ken whaur they reside.

'And Pluto's whaur thi Latin slept,
the Akkadian and thi Greek;
and Sedna's whaur thi tales werr kept
thi plains tribes yaised tae speak.'

'But sey mair o wir lunar lair,
these archives o thi damned:
wi whame dae we this exile share,
wi whame hae we been crammed?

'Thi Magyars and thi Catalans,
thi Bulgars and Walloons –
wee nations wi still sma'er chance
o lastin – got thi Mune.'

'And whit about wir ither tongues,   ·
thi Gaelic and thi Welsh?'
'See whaur thon crash-site's spilled uts lungs?
They're drooned withoot a squelch.'

And wi that soond thi gless aa fell,
thi drones swaarmed in, and in that mell,
pushed thru thi exit fae that cell,
        thi poet loupt.
He thocht he heard a yelled, 'Farewell!'
        Syne aa wiz coupt.

Ejectit fae thi Biblioglobe
he tumblet doon thi lunar slope
and landit wi a kick and grope
        in a sea o dust
that micht content a hydrophobe –
        aa croak and crust.

And floondirt in thi flinders there
nor flochtin, sinkin, findin air
that he could tak and in despair
     crehd oot fur help –
at whilk a curious temerair
     cemm at a skelp.

This wiz a hauf-screpped-oot pirogue
mair fuhl o holes than a gowfin brogue
in which twa beardy-wierdy rogues
     sat up lyk skuas
and entered intae this collogue
     wi braith lyk brewers:

'Ma brither in thi habbie, hail.
Ye've learnt tae soom in Lethe's skail
whaur nane can pass and aa maun fail
     eventually –
tho rebels grab a raft and sail
     lyk him and me.'

'Oor craft's in sair need o a bail,
ut's rudderless and hiz nae timmers,
jist paper clipped wi fingernails,
uts mast's a pen. But tho nocht's grimmer
          nor this silent sea
jist lease us oan wir mony limmers
     and we sall face thi gales
lyk Gaels in birlinns, save aa swimmers,
     and spear thi whitest whales –
          fur free.'

'Dye ken ye're sailin oan thi mune
whaur ony whales wad likely be
leviathans o dust whas froons
wad rax far langer than Glenshee?'

'An inkpot fur Mjollnir and
a quill fur a harpoon,
we'll hook em beh thi balls, sir, and
we'll dang thir fizzogs doon.'

gowfin: golfing; *collogue:* conversation; *soom:* swim; *lease us on:* an expression of
affection for something; *limmers:* lovers.

'Dye ken there's niver hope o port?
We're poems in a sea o prose:
whaur Oblivion fishes fur his sport:
ye'll breathe nae Ayr, nor smell Montrose.'

'A dictionair fur oor guitar
a plooshare fur oor spoon
thigither we'll loup ayont thi bar
and sing beh thi licht o thi...'

                                   'Yird.'

'Absurd!
But we'll sing beh thi licht o thi yird.'

SHANTY OF THE SAILORS' MOON

Mare Silentium
is whaur aa sowels at last dae come
whas life wiz spent upon
thi silent craft o song
tae sail awa sae dumb
(*Mare Silentium*)
we sail awa sae dumb

Layin thi keels o phrase
or sailin skeely thru the waves
that waash ower in crazy praise
until oor time is duin
and we sail tae kingdom come
(*Mare Silentium*)
we sail tae kingdom come

Oceans o lusty sang
atween thi lends o ports we panged
until thi saut they crehd
garred aa thi seas rin dreh
whaur we noo sail sae numb
(*Mare Silentium*)
we sail awa sae dumb

loup: leap; *skeely:* skilful; *lends:* thighs; panged: packed; *saut:* salt.

99

Tarrin thi stanza's hull
barque or ark, we tack or scull
nae hope o haven here
and sae nae need tae steer
jist sail tae kingdom come
(*Mare Silentium*)
we sail tae kingdom come

Yirth wi her bonny sash
looks doon upon a sea o ash
whaur aa ships come tae wreck
sae we waulk an eemis deck
and sail awa sae dumb
(*Mare Silentium*)
we sail tae kingdom come

eemis: unsteady.

BAD SHAMAN BLUES

The woman said, 'You have come from far away. Yet, I am obliged to send you back.' And she breathed on me three times. As she was breathing I began to recognise the place.

from the account of the shaman SEREPTIE,
Shamanic Voices, ed. John Halifax

Air Sibir as Shamanic Flight

Direction doesn't matter – taiga's
relentless ringworm forests; lakes
we cross for hours, beside which tigers
with phosphor coats await their Blakes;
east, west, up, down – are each negated
by this old plane's decor: belated
ill-fitting tan wallpaper fills
it to and from its windowsills;
families perch their weekend shopping
on knees amid the flopping seats,
the frequent vodka and boiled sweets –
and if you take to Ural-hopping
or not, this flight's a long strange trip
that takes us all from blip to blip.

In which I see the way I travel
is equal to the way I live:
inept, withdrawn, and half-unravelled,
too full of neediness to give;
barely witnessed seeing fiercely,
never heard or very nearly.
To such a shaman still belongs
all partial and irrational songs.
The purview that the travel purist
obtains through months of rooting down –
all well-earned insights – I renounce.
I am content to be the tourist
who finds home in that other place
with cyphers crawling on its face.

That we approach our destination
is clear from shudderings and groans
as though the plane gets premonitions
now that we near the spirit zones.
Instead of donning psychic armour,
I'm thinking I'd once claimed the glamour
of unknown cities hits your brain
with first love's force. 'So you'd regain
your youth by travel?' asked that devil's

advocate AKA a friend –
not what I'd thought of as my end;
but neither is this far from level
half-swoop, half-swooning down through air –
as threatened hearts applaud, we're here.

In retrospect the shack for baggage,
the cage and then the carousel,
should each have served as grinding presage
that all indeed might not be well.
But such relief at such a landing
had addled keener understanding.
The runway filled with evening light:
that orange chill, the fading flight,
the brief belief we'd reached Siberia –
conspiring to dismiss those fears
the time zones crossed were deeper: years
of jumping to a jammed interior
of thought, not just a continent.
So this was what Siberia meant.

The Grumbling Box Problem

A television shows me its most intimate cartoons, the ones in which the ages and the genders of the somersaulting participants mutate constantly, pinning me to the bracken carcass of the hotel's best shoddy furniture. It's very late somewhere in the world my inner ear can't place; even how high up the building this is is unsettled by the jetlag. I appear to be in a narrow pod being shown rage doilies, Rorschach upholstery, wallpaper lingerie. I gaze at them for a long transgressive moment not following not only a single word but a single note of the accompanying plastic balalaikan timpani-eats-piano soundtrack. After a while I realise I am in bed and all the lights are out apart from the dirty snow light at the centre of the continental night and I also realise I am being muttered to. From some point in the room the dancing dots of vitamin-deficient vision prevent me from making out, someone is muttering to me in a voice so indistinct I can't even establish whether or not it is Russian or an aboriginal language: Chuvash, Khant, Tuvan, Yakut. I lie there for another of your Earth minutes. The voice drones on, apparently exterior to my fizzing cranium. I check I have not left the television on. I pull the plug from the wall like a rotten tooth on string just in case. The muttering is replaced by an indistinct snatch of music: one of those frozen blocks exported to Phil Spector to construct the Wall of Sound. No single instrument is distinguishable, but the noise draws me to a sort of cabinet by the head of the bed. I don't remember seeing this before but it looks like a giant radio. It has clacky controls apparently for stations and frequencies, a dial possibly for volume, and a number of switches, bulgy lights (off), and grilles of indefinite function. The voice has resumed, but when I clack, twist and flick, nothing appears to happen. I put my ear to one of the grilles, but cannot confirm that the grumbling is actually coming from this machine. I speak into another one of the grilles, 'Please stop this incessant noise.' I stare at it as though it's the TV and some message will be displayed on it. The lights continue not to flash. I try to move it to find the power source but either it's too heavy or it's attached to the wall. After a while I lie down again, whereupon there is another short outburst of music, possibly the same as before. The voice continues to grumble into my wax-encumbered ear, apparently telling me all its problems, or perhaps telling me all my problems, or possibly all the problems that have afflicted this floating city since it was founded in the middle of absolutely nothing a little over a hundred years ago. No, it is not like Middlesbrough. Perhaps I am listening to the groaning complaint of the countless exiles and prisoners whose camps' remains remain around us in the vast coldness of the night. Perhaps if I concentrate I will be able to distinguish Dostoevsky muttering from Omsk, or Mandelstam on his way to Kamchatka, or someone whose name I do not know, whose crime even they did not know, whose next thought is completely unknown, whose only recourse is this word and this word and this next word I still cannot make out. Perhaps I am listening to the ground itself, grudgingly defrosting for the spring that begins tomorrow morning wherever that is. Perhaps this will go on all night. It does.

Good Morning Novosibirsk!

From the heightened window
of my Intourist pod
the city is spread like a frozen honey
beneath a sun's broad morning knife
its crystals glinting back from

the stubby blocks and the River Ob
and grey snow which has declared itself
unmeltable and gathered in
sullen adolescent groups
the wrong side of anything.

The cold dries out my face and its
fungoid interior. My nipples flake
and fall from my chest.
Each hair uncoils like a fever
and rehearses being beard.

We board a shabby-curtained bus
and ride across the meandering water
past three barber pole chimneys
manufacturing intercontinental gripe
and we look at small towers built from names,

memorials for the great Patriotic War.
Children clap their guns and steam;
a golden Lenin poses for
the millions who can't be wrong
because they're dead.

The hole in my shoe laps greedily
at potato-flavoured slush.
Adrenalin slows to a thixotropic slur,
my spine feels like an AK-47
which has jammed.

The Bridge Across the River Ob

In echteen hundert and ninety one
McGonagall's work wiz niver done;
in addition tae writin aboot ivry bloody battle
therr werr numerous engineerin feats he also hud tae tackle,
but thi wan he wiz oblivious of wiz a maist momentous joab:
thi bridge across thi River Ob.

Since this iz thi third langest river in thi world
ut wiz a proaject that got Chief Engineer Garin's taes aa curled,
and thi Czar's navvies objectit tae his scheme
and muttirt constructions that micht huv been obscene.

It wiz certainly a cauld and obdurate spectacle
But Chief Engineer Garin said, 'Brave boys, this may be an obstacle
but the surrounding bogs are comparatively pretty,
so oblige me and I'll design you a Siberian city,
and we shall call it Novosibirsk,
and one day it may become as big as Thirsk.'

Sae they set to and completit thir girdered bridge
and the Express rowled across it wi an Imperial carriage.
The railway rins fae Moscow tae obscure Vladivostok
and taks six deys tae get there, which must come as a shock
tae those yaised tae traivellin beh GNER,
a mair Oblomovistic set o chuffers that dinnae gae sae far.
And wance ut gets tae thi end o the track
they turn thi trenn roond, and ut comes richt back.

And Novisibirsk wiz built oot ae logs
which they obviously foond growein jist next tae thi bogs,
and obtains in thi centre o Russia tae this day
tho thi cauld, ye micht think, wid mak thi people rin away,
but thi semm is observably no true o Perth
which wad itherwise be given a considerable berth,
fur thi factor unitin baith oblast and nation
is often no faith, but plain obstipation.

We tend tae say we're brave when we're jist bein obstinate
and thi mair obtuse amang us ur mair like a winnet,
and when they shid gee up thir hame, joab or hobby
they cling til thir roots like a sticky wee jobby.
But thi citizens o Novosibirsk ur courageous and noble
and laugh in Winter's icy teeth, and dinna gee an obol.

Sae beautiful River Ob, sae broad and fleet,
Eh hope ye niver cheenge yir course, and mak thi bridge obsolete;
and metallic brig that straddles thi Ob,
may meh verse aboot you mak grown men sob.

By the Road to Akademgorodok

By the road to Akademgorodok
rows of little chimneys protrude
from the blasted defrosting earth, and mark
the stores for last year's produce.
> *now the deeper freeze of permafrost's*
> *reheating at our touch*

Potatoes snooze in these rooms, displaced
but honoured, like Kirghiz princesses: they dream
on long beds in their brown-walled izbas
with trestle tables spread before them.
> *with the DNA of mammoths like*
> *a thighbone in their clutch*

I can hear their vodka-soaked telephones
ringing: hear them grumbling, Who has called
at this time of year? It's Uncle Joe.
He always calls in case the harvest fails.
> *though all the bones he buried here*
> *should fertilise the soil*

They are potato princesses, they have rare
ways of listening; they're not scared
of anything he says or promises,
and they will intercede for us.
> *if the permafrost's foundations fall*
> *they'll tell us where there's oil*

Novosibirskaya Skazka

Once, when the winter was hanging
its stockings in the trees
and all its sheets had blown
from the rigid birdclaws of the clothes pegs
and lay across the exhausted grass,

and every river had frozen so thick
from mouth to spring that you could pick
it up and wave it like a piece of lightning
to conduct the music of the children's breath
as they hurried from potato to potato,

and they dressed each one in a splendid jacket
made from all the letters of the alphabet
you cannot use in winter
because your teeth have stuck to
a lump of sugar – all the letters' legs

entwined like mohair or the wigs
made by an industry of earwigs from
the hairs inside the ears of doctors
especially warm from the heartbeats
passing up their stethoscopes like colic,

all the fretting care for children
hungry for the *skazki* that I alone,
Viktor, burning on the taiga
with vodka and angina, can produce...
Where was I, and where was my accordion?

Anyway, and it certainly happened once
while the bears sat in the woods
with shot glasses in their eyes,
posing as astronomers – I was poised
with ten fingers entangled in a typewriter,

sewing words into blouses
for all brave potatoes when
the seven white swans of steam
gliding on the surface of my porridge
announced that it was time to scry.

Slipping into two slack-stringed guitars
I skated like a glazed lorry, jack-
knifing at the prognosticating pot,
But before I could pebbledash the door,
hurling and harling with grey abandon,

a cockroach with a red moustache
crawled under the doorframe and said,
'I have evaded claw-jousting cats
to bring you this warning:
beware the obedience of children.

'They will dine on foreign influence
as I dine on the faeces of mice.
At present they carry nightingales
unharmed in their mouths,
but when they grow up they will kill you.'

I seized my ladle painted with uranium flowers
and mashed it, then sat, scooping out
a dollop of my brain, and firing it,
and another, splat by slushy splat,
against the peeling treebark of my shack.

Skazka, skazki: fairytale, tales; *scry:* read the future, often done in *skazki* by
flinging porridge at a door.

Hangover Thursday

It's Hangover Thursday and I have got
two telephones embedded on either side
of my shivering spine.

They are ivory coloured, and the ear-bowls
and mouth-bowls are like halves of eggs
and they ring constantly.

On one line is Stalin and on the other Pasternak:
they need me in their bickering, to talk
to each other through.

'Tell him I never meant for Mandelstam to die –
I thought he was tougher than that.'
'Tell him to fuck himself, I'm dead.'

'And by the way you must pack instantly:
you're leaving.' I hang up and rush downstairs
but the bus has gone.

Thoughts of last night's Nestlé reps churn and return:
grim twins in Bermuda shorts, skinless chipmunks dancing,
cranberry vodka.

'You'll need to catch a cab,' says Pasternak
but I don't hear the destination properly,
so drag my bags through *slyatka*

into a schoolyard where there is
the skeleton of a reindeer built from steel tubules:
it sits in the snow and Stalin tells me

'That is your soul.' I drag my suitcase to
another school and the plastic bag inside my shoe
fills up with slush.

I sit in the classroom but can't hear the lesson
because the phones are ringing constantly
with their questions:

'What has a sheepskin but no ribs?'
'Why has the Tsar's hat no seams, the birch hut
no windows, the bottle no cork?'

'Why are there two nations in the one house?'
'Why are there two wines in one cask?'
I can't answer, because

my head feels like a silver barrel full
of golden drink. 'Good,' says Pasternak,
'If you work it hard you'll get a hen.'

slyatka: slush.

The Professor of Tiny Books

The Professor of Tiny Books has discovered
a thriving city of demons alive within
the printed word though he won't say which one.

Barabashkagrad, he lectures, is like a mirror
of our city, and here he sings that anthem
he has heard employing microphones

that focus with precision on a single descender.
He stamps about the stage and slaps a devilish
but imaginary accordion. The tune is very like

that anthem he performed an hour ago
which he composed for the town's new underground,
unaccountably rejected by the authorities.

The Urals, he now argues, are a mirror
so that the Russias of the east and west
reflect each other almost exactly, except for

certain officials magically replaced
by grossly magnified demonic counterparts
only his precisely aligned lenses reveal.

This malign infestation can be countered by him
rewriting the whole of Russian literature
in progressively tinier books (and here

his brandishing of Pushkin between pincers
implies our search can narrow to
the poems), until the gravitational pull

of that single letter becomes so strong (and now
his emphasis implies a focus on the fly sound
'ж' – appropriate for lordlings of corruption),

ж: *jeh*, pronounced like the 's' in 'measure': the sound Russians ascribe to
a buzzing fly.

that no one from the infernal city can escape.
Next he shows histology slides suggesting
gulags for the barabashky-apparatchniks

now loose could be established in the livers
of loyal former party members, good Christians,
and here he's minded of an anthem from his youth...

Bad Shaman Blues

Well ma ma bought me a bodhran but Eh cannae keep thi beat
and when Eh see a sickie kiddie Eh jist stert tae greet –
Eh've gote thi bad shaman blues (bad shaman blues).
Eh tak ma magic mushrooms and begin tae fleh
but then Eh croodle in thi corner while meh harnies freh,
coz that's thi bad shaman blues (yeah that's thi bad shaman blues).
Well aa guid people wi-ah porridge in yir theghs
get up and gang tae work
while Eh leh here and waatch thi crab-sun rehz
coz Eh am jist a jerk.
And that's thi mewly droolin pewly foolin
bad shaman blues
yeah that's thi grown man yelpin poor Van Helsin
bad shaman blues.

Well some people think Eh'm evil but they huvnae gote a clue
coz at thi furst apparition Eh jist weeja tae thi loo –
Eh've gote thi bad shaman poos (bad shaman poos).
And Eh mak ut tae thi bathroom in ma sleepin bag
whaur thi knotholes in thi flairboards they continue tae nag
'Ye've gote thi bad shaman blues' (bad shaman blues).
Aa guid people wi pehs fur ehz
ut's time tae stoap fur lunch
Eh'll tell ye nae truths and Eh'll tell ye nae lehs
Eh'm whit thi monsters munch.
Coz that's thi pukey rooky plukey stookie
bad shaman blues
yeah that's thi black-ah mass and Quatermassin
bad shaman blues.

Well Eh see thi dots and spirals and Eh waant tae hide
Eh've gote three white feathirs that'll smother meh pride
cause that's whit bad shamans use (bad shamans use).
Doon below thi river whaur thi auld queen sits
see me queuein fir a stewin lyk a hopeless wee shit
coz that's whit bad shamans do (yeah that's whit bad shamans do).

Well aa guid people wi sliders fur spines
drehv aff and pick up yir kids
cause thi wey Eh huvtae pey meh lehbrury fines
meh pants ur fuhl o skids.
But that's thi tottery snortery, toss him oot thi coterie
bad shaman blues,
yeah that's thi Scooby Gang and Whovian, act lyk you're Venusian
bad shaman blues.

Well Eh meet a lot o people wi sticks fur heids
and a lot o them ur nutters and a few ur deid
but that's thi bad shaman blues (bad shaman blues).
And hoo thi hell's a gimp lyk me a-gonnae help a man
wha's soul's an ell o charcoal and ut jist fell in thi sand?
but that's whit bad shamans do (yeah that's whit bad shamans do).
Aa guid people wi yir heids a-fuhl o mince
get oot and beh some tat
while Eh think things that mak thi spiders wince
and act lyk Eh'm a bat.
Coz that's thi moanin groanin helpline phonin
bad shaman blues,
yeah that's thi Mulder and Scully, older than Oor Wullie
bad shaman blues.

A lot o weemen blame me fur behaviour beh thir ex-es
Eh'm itherwise an oabject o disdain fur baith thi sexes –
that's jist thi bad shaman blues (it's jist thi bad shaman blues).
Eh like tae think it helps tae write yir symptoms doon
but Eh feel lyk Eh'm thi public fiss of Eccles thi Goon
sae Eh scrieve these bad shaman blues (scrieve these bad shaman blues).
Aa guid people wi hough fur herts
jist get yirsels tae sleep
Eh've a vigil set wi Virgil whaur thi Devil farts
that Eh'm too feart tae keep.
But that's the violet-shrinkin, cannae stop thinkin
bad shaman blues
ut's jist thi Buffy-lovin, Tufty-clubbin
bad shaman blues.

(diminuendo)

It's thi chittery flittery wittery skittery
bad shaman blues
it's the shamble-lyk-a-shot-stirk, Randall and-ah Hopkirk
bad shaman blues
thi hokum-frichtenin, scrotum-tichtenin
bad shaman blues
thi lab-rat yellow, Abbot and Costello
bad shaman blues

bad shaman blues
bad shaman blues
bad shaman blues

who's bad?

The Descent to Moscow

Descending through the clouds to Moscow
is like the hope that in the deeps
of Saturn's gases might be Glasgow;
or coming down from stubborn trips:
just as you look on what resembles
a level steppe, the brain dissembles –
you're through into another grey
where still more un-lands stretch away,
so far within the air's foundations
the pressure builds up to believe
this is beneath the normal life;
that here be turbulent crustaceans
with Moscow's root within their claw –
till clouds clear on the runway's maw.

It's like the drop into the Metro:
how fast the escalators fall
between those globes that cast their retro
light on dark wood, the people's marble halls.
My last time here that fall seemed faster,
the lights all cast a quicker lustre –
and so we pass between the clouds.
Familiarity's a shroud
across the face of any city
including this, so redolent
it's one colossal fingerprint
accused of murder and of beauty.
And so to see it one more time
as duller seems a petty crime.

I'm peering at Mendeleevskaya's
periodic chandeliers
and thinking how I'd be a liar
to say sight sharpens with the years,
but this diminished misdemeanour
perversely makes the problem plainer:
there is a genre hidden in
these instants like Erato's twin.
That opening that's stunned, unknowing,

where bookshops in the underpass
taste homely and as strange as *kvas*;
that first arrival, as mind-blowing
as first love – travel stops, defined:
it's in its blink we see we're blind.

We know this moment that's before us
with love or chemicals becomes
eternal – we should be its chorus,
except, like Coleridge, we're dumb.
and so I climb out at the Kremlin
where once some younger strophes, trembling,
tried to transfer this inmost whorl
of Russia's print: today the world
revolves around these antistrophes'
hangover, jetlag-spiked, and thus
the Flame and Zhukov seem a fuss;
Red Square's weird domes are dusty trophies
I once collected – now I bore
still eager friends with tourist lore.

But part of me is still descending –
from that high cloud-occluded dome,
from hour-long rivers, unrelenting
roadlessness – I'm still coming home
through this succession of the membranes,
hallucinations of remembrance
and reconfronted detail: how
those green and yellow diamonds glowed
as though the domes were flies on acid;
the way a children's clothing store
and the Lubyanka form one square;
and how the waitress stood in tacit
disdain when we delayed in GUM –
all wrapped in that metallic gloom.

Take notes on every mental photo
hound every fragmentary phrase,
you still won't know where instants go to:
no facts admit us to that place.
Perhaps I'm better lost in tunnels,
between things in the Metro's ginnels;

the orbit entered underground
gives hints where home can't quite be found:
this view of the adjoining *droshky*
where clothes are almost out of style
and dozing faces never smile;
those station names in muttered Russki;
the holy drunk these childish cops
eject – here is its small eclipse.

A safety we call indecision's
made tolerable by the way
these T-shirt's English lacks precision,
or ads for *cheryomushky*
get misread as the Shostakovich
opera with its hand-in-glovich
home-dealing bureaucrats. This mesh
of mistakes' kinships is so rich
the sense of scissors that has hovered
over these threads is set aside
for the duration of this ride,
Instantinople is recovered,
until its gates are once more breached –
since Park Kultury has been reached.

And lunch has culture with eight bells on:
it's with an editor who wants
to feast us like new writing's Nelson
upon a floating restaurant.
We sailed the droog ship Neurasthena
last night, so pause – then I see Lena
pass through the rumbling portico,
who showed me Moscow years ago
when every street sign seemed hermetic –
my last night here we danced and ate
great Georgian fare, inebriate
again (that same cuisine's emetic
potential's threatened here). We kiss
each other's smaller, older face.

It's clear I'm endlessly arriving
without the brains to be arrived:
though that may feel the same as leaving

I now know that I've never left,
for meeting Lena sets in action
time's grinning muscle – that contraction
defines these second visit blues
as tidal, trading friends with loss
just like our appetite's revival:
down bean-paste deltas, past Fort Lamb,
through fennel meadows to the calm
that Georgian reds provide – arrival
not as recovery of youth
but letting loose its types of truth.

We spurn a retrograde returning
to our hotel by Metro for
a riverboat, its more discerning
completion of our orbit's score.
Not-Boring Park; that science building's
gold *Soyuz* top; the long loop yielding
Vesodka views knee-deep in trees;
another *piva*, at our ease...
the epode to all that descending
is coming back's more like a scar:
you stroke it to be reassured.
Though landing is a kind of ending
it's not the healing but the wound
you're touching till you touch the ground.

THE MINISTRY OF DOUBT

Jesus said to his disciples, 'Compare me to something and tell me what I am like.'

Simon Peter said to him, 'You are like a just messenger.'

Matthew said to him, 'You are like a wise philosopher.'

Thomas said to him, 'Teacher, my mouth is utterly unable to say what you are like.'

FROM *The Gospel of Thomas*

Sri Ganesh Tyres

As the taxi is shouldering its way between mustard-coloured motorised rickshaws, mopeds and other sleek bulbous white Ambassadors, I see a man rolling a huge tyre down the main street. It's as tall as him, and he's rolling it past a wall covered in faded scripture in blue and red writing, one section in English, one in Tamil. We pass too quickly for me to recognise the text, but something sufficiently religious sufficiently deep inside me acknowledges it. Later I work out it's the Thousand Lights Mosque.

The man looks as though he's leisurely pursuing a large vehicle which is somehow continuing with only three wheels; he looks as though the truck he was once driving has been eroded over thousands of miles, leaving him only this remnant to complete his journey with. I keep seeing this man and this tyre, or this man with a different tyre, or this tyre with a different man, or some other combination, till in my sleep I imagine one man rolling another man down the street, or large tyres strolling around in pairs, like the bases of giant phantom motorcycles. Their tread is made up of dark acknowledged scripture.

Later I am driven round the corner, and pass Sri Ganesh Tyres, a little frontage piled high with circular rubber ziggurats like the sloughed skins of bathing elephants.

Kapalishvara

The splay-wheeled juggernaut
is parked down a sidestreet,
its turquoise pillars supporting

a thirty foot pyramid of gods,
though its wood-slat tiers
are dwarfed by the gopura

over the temple entrance –
that mound of holy termites,
that technicolour hive of deities.

Shoeless in the courtyard,
I hardly notice
the lingam in its gate

till a family come through,
the women's ankles chinking
with little chains,

and proceed to worship
what I'd just gauped at,
my feet in a warm puddle.

An old man takes me round
the low bepostered shrines –
we stand, considering

the old tree where
Shiva turned Parvati into
a mayil or peahen because

she'd been distracted by a
peacock from her lord –
except of course, he explains,

this isn't the original site
so that can't exactly be
the original tree.

The wooden animals from
the annual procession are stacked
like carnival creatures

in a shed-full of shadows
their painter comes out from
hot-chested and chatty

about me scribbling as
my guide extracts rupees
and sterling for

narrating how san thome
cathedral had claimed
this temple's prime location   ,

on the ocean front
but how easily it has
rerooted itself here.

I retrieve my shoes but am
reluctant to put them on:
something more has been displaced.

Mathura

No matter how carefully they repeat it
I can't tell the time on the ten hour
stainless steel clock-plate of my
mini-meal in the low-roofed restaurant.
It's too light brown and dim in here
and I'm too hungry for such gradations.

Does the puri hand point to something
past spinach dish, or is it time for sambar?
Is it dhal past pappadom yet? I feel I'm in
the polished wooden workings
of some delicious recorder with these pillars
in the centre, each one elephant-leg-thick.

Meanwhile the steamed rice seconds pile up
and it still doesn't seem to be time for curd.
I give myself up as we all do to the advance,
the right hand's dance across the disc
that heats noon's palate then cools it off
towards the afternoon. Until the chilli doughnut.

While Rathi and Prasanna compare
the hours on a Kerala plate with those
of Tamil Nadu, I try to remove from my nose
the fragment of an instant, the name of which
has evaded both my brain and mouth,
and gaze at the tops of the caramel pillars:

they have four tiers of glass tubes, frilled
and ascending concentrically to
the creamy roof of the cool and bustling room.
They look like the pleated layered skirts
of classical goddesses, swirling up
Monroe-style, into unchanging light.

An Informationist Is Shown Around the Government Museum

Hand of a Roman, heart of a Dravidian

At the start he runs off to get his laser
instead of touching the darkened stone

between the feet of the female statues
is the shape of the temple gate

his wife and daughter hover in
the first room as he indicates

the hand and the joints of the fingers
dictate the proportions of body and face

I don't need to copy this down
I can use his website later

the eyes are the last to be carved
so God doesn't see the carver

forty years old, a PhD student in
Archaeology who gets by as a guide

sixteen knots protect the secrecy
of the wealth of the family

his son appears between the sati stones
and the slab depicting the Buddha's stupa

everything in fives or sevens
indicating deeds or virtues

outside, between the crumbling red-bricks
cotton is blown through scaffolding

the mnemonics of
the encyclopaedic eye

before the Chola bronzes
in 101 degrees he flags

subduing evil by dancing on a dwarf
Nataraja bestows grace on the world

and drinks from my water without
letting the bottle touch his lips.

General Epistle of Thomas

He had a garland on his chest,
a strong bow in his grip,
arrow already chosen,
and he asked which way
the elephant went
with an arrow buried in its side.

KAPILAR (trans. A.K. Ramanujan)

Thomas Didymus, apostle of doubt, to the strangers
who may be living peaceably or at war throughout
the hills and forests, plains and wastes and seashores
in Mylapore, Mamallapuram and in Gingee,
in Kanchipuram, Tiruvannamallai and Pondicherry,
those unelected through any foreknowledge
of the Lord, nevertheless, Grace unto you.
You have your faith as I lack mine;
you have searched out the Spirit diligently
as you have searched out the honey and the mango
and the jackfruit, as you search out those clouds that
like the lips of angels suck rain from the sea
to succour you, and you have waited
with the patience I could not muster when my Lord
was reported found, green in the desert as the palai tree.
I, who have arrived among you like the fish
caught up in the cheeks of the angels and spat forth;
like the weed which springs up between the toes
of the fishermen waiting for their tide, patient as
the neytal, blue lily of the shoreline; I am like
a living stone which cries out to the pilgrim
in the desert's rage; I am like the grooves
worked in that stone by the thirsty at prayer;
I am like the cross cut in that stone by one
who would mark his desolation with a scar: here it is.
Let me ask you, Poet of the Fingers Round a Bow,
how can I come close to Him whom I have doubted,
his side-wound like a lotus in the water
that I drowned with one bloody hand? Let me ask you,
Poet of the Ploughman With a Single Plough,
how long must my heart wait, frantic for him?

My followers say the rock gave birth to water
and drink from its dirty spring, but I have heard
that in the hills where hunters go there is a flower
red as my Lord's blood and rich in honey. I will go
where the kurinci blossoms and hide my hand.
And therefore I leave you to love one another
without faith in the life or lives to come,
love one another in the only moment in which
we know our failings make us loveable to God.

Adda

All day I've been a penguin in the library,
telling kids how those birds form a shuffling mass,
like seed-pods on the coldest sunflower:
iceflower of the Southern floes.
I've been explaining how the circle churns
to make outsiders, how each bird spends
a moment in the white petals of that blast,
and this is how I'd like to see their city.

Instead I've been rushed from boiling shade
to shade, drunk *Thumbs Up* in the compound,
and gazed at Kolkatta's grimy shimmer past the glass:
all day I've been the emperor of air-conditioning.

Later, I sit on the verandah of the Director's flat
and discuss the rain that's suddenly, deafeningly
falling on the palm-leaves and the car-tops.
It's dark now, the lightning emitted from
the underside of clouds needles at bicyclists;
the day's heat is sawn through by the teeth
of rain, the sharpness of the shower.
This is *Kaalbaishakhi*, the April Norwester.

Sarika says there is a season pinched between
Rainy and Autumn called *Sarat*, bright, not hot –
better for visiting. But I love this whetted weather
as much as her recarving of my quartered year:

it's like the way that mood-words want to be
untranslatable, a dictionary of difference:
hiraeth, honfibu, fortwursteln, suadade –
new seasons in the mind –
and *abhiman*, a word she tells me means
'pride' in Hindi, but in Bangla it expands,
like a blossom in the rain, into this sulking
as at something mistakenly withheld.

Adda: (pronounced *urda*) informed informal chat.

Howrah Kabitika

A motorbike covered in sacking is dragged past
to be posted. Men roll oildrums down
the road between the platforms. The soft
persistence of the beggars is like sweat:
a legless boy tapping at my calf;
an old woman so small she reaches the base
of my ribs, propelling herself with a stick worn
to a kind of hornshape by her hand;
a woman with an infant sleeping through
the quiet brow-sweep process of pleading
and rejection. Already I am drenched in pity.

*

In the AC Carriage

A boy, the size of two rupees,
clutching a packet of chocolate biscuits
and wearing sandals with a squeak in each heel,
is snatched by parents from the path
of chai and paper chanters.

*

Lemon Tea Kabitika

small plastic cup and not
the clay ones shattered in
their orange hundreds in between the rails
like brittle fingernail goodbyes

lemon sweet but salty too
as thick as tears
the tongue-imagined flakes as big as teeth
dissolving in a dragged-on urn

cha lemoo cha

133

Santiniketan

Dark on the concrete porch with Debanjan's professor
in a deckchair chatting quietly beneath
the increasing silence of the trees, but not so dark
I couldn't see the high branches and the bats'
darker blue blades against the welling blue milk
of the silent starless sky, the space between
each word and its neighbour growing longer
like a town becoming countryside until
we were walking home along the avenue
of huge trees and I saw someone
smoking in the field, so dark now it was just
the cold tip of their cigarette just beyond
where the tailor had stood with his table below
the branches to repair the passers-bys' clothing
but there was another, dancing perhaps
or waving lazily becoming my first
fireflies and then there were
uncertain constellations of them, fireflies all the way
back beside the broad canal until
we came upon a crowd with ropes
taut by the bend where the truck had slipped
and fallen on one shoulder spilling all
its earthy rubble on the lawn and
it seemed as though we too should haul on
the wrist-thick ropes in pitcher darkness now
until we couldn't tell but felt the poise
of the almost-decided, half-right truck
and then it thudded back with such
determination that it threw us all
back in our separate directions and
Debanjan and I went on to Prantik
never knowing that the broken-necked poor driver's
ghost came blowing back with us and drank
molasses whisky and listened to us chat
and lay upon the spare bed in my room
and watched the ceiling fan's brown blades
spin slowly to cessation.

Santhal Shop

Spun on that slow wheel of generations'
knack and nous and never glazed:
the blue-striped cool round interlocking
houses and courtyards of mud
that one clan fills precisely;

ovens rising like lava bubbles, cut
to admit the copper skillet, cook
and architect arranging
heat and shade in demilunes;
set by the proper palms up which

a son offered to collect the sap
brewed into the drink we were
too busy finding to wait for fresh,
so drove past scattered easy huts
in the growing dusk;

past tattered straw goddesses
they'd fished out from the rivers after
Bolpur's's Tushu Porob
and set up under trees to view the sunset.
And in one courtyard found

an amused grandma whose sleepy child
fetched the cloudy white *taari*
much diluted for the city boys
who sat beneath the palms and trees
conjoining in the glowing dark;

and I thought of the cave of shop
where we'd stopped to ask
for our elixir: how it seemed
a tilting wall of jars, two insect wings
of glass with the shopkeeper's head

shaking between them; how
there seemed to be no contents in them,
the more I tried to remember
their dusty little globes
grew emptier and emptier

as though containing air
from further and further north,
higher juggings with cold stars,
small mountain peaks of 'Breathe Me'
I found myself exhaling

in the dark courtyard with
the grandma and the child and my friends,
all of us drinking in and breathing out
the distances between tribe and town,
city and continent and star.

GEORGIOUPOLICS

Embrace me then, ye Hills, and close me in...

WORDSWORTH,
'Home at Grasmere'

Why I am here is not the point.

W.S. GRAHAM,
'In the Street of Knives'

The Measure

When I make myself porridge I always use
this small glazed cup from Crete
to measure out the portions: oats,
soya milk, water. If, once the bowl

is turning in the microwave, I invert the cup,
its base becomes a narrow belt
from which the bulge of hips in a tight skirt
splays and narrows just above the knees.

It's the stunned brown earth of a hillside in
the August shade, all meat and cinnamon,
but sheened, made shell upon my lips
as though the sea has mothered it for years.

It has a seeping dark horizon band
around it where it gathers, another where
its mouth expands to plant
a milky rim on the ply worktop.

I didn't buy it – my wife did that
a decade before we'd met. I didn't choose
the towns that now appear to shape it
as they shape the river whose banks make clay:

Emprosneros, that girdles springs in the hills;
Vrisses, that grips the water's flanks
with eucalyptus and the smell of spitted lamb;
and Georgioupouli, opened to the bay.

I never saw myself, photoing the negative space
between the occipital dome of the mosque
and the long-masted Venetian lighthouse;
eating on the harbour's curve at Chania

the same yoghurt and honey tanged with thyme
that I spoon into my breakfast bowl.
I never did a thing to make it happen,
so why do I measure out oats from this cup?

Old Bookshop, Chania

This angle to our days that always sends
us through like sunlight when we'd rather sit
in each encountered hour, inhabit it
the way we do its memory, which tends
to sketch out letters in old alphabets,
sometimes backwards, or on that dusty lens
the sideboard lost, or with those unbought pens
we clicked in stationers, their graded sets.
Step into the store down those bone-bright streets,
its shade triangle which has waited since
the Thirties till you scan those spines in Greek
you'd hoped to read by now. Relax, and once
you're sure which notebook (narrow feint), how thick
the nib (too fine), then tilt them and begin.

Boy with Duck and Apple

(Rethymnon Archaeological Museum)

She wouldn't let me sketch the headless boy
who has a duck tucked under one arm,
an apple in the other hand as though
these were bat and ball in some lost game.

Presumably he wasn't catalogued
as fully as the other statues and
my drawing, dreadful as it was, could stand
as rival record, though, like him, one-legged.

But I prefer to speculate there were
arcaner motives here: a local cult
who argued that the duck and not the serpent
caused the Fall, a vocal fowl whose fault's

avenged in cypher by this marble Abel:
choked by sin's fruit, and roasted for the table.

I feel the stern attendant watch my eyes
and wonder which ephebe I'll memorise.

Revithia

I free revithia, nut-sharp nodes
from solo, nearly sea-green pods,
and love how tones evade our terms,
the way that faces lose their names
returning to this wrist of beach:
we almost smile or nearly touch.

The stalks are drying leaf to root,
until they nearly match their fruit
or that small bird that starts to hop
among the loungers for our scraps.

The bird won't settle on the stone
that's blinded by the evening sun;
my daughter points a brilliance out
I'm almost sure that she'll forget.

We keep the plastic soldier that
we found here, throwing a grenade
that's nearly chickpea-shaped, whose face,
distorted by the cheap mould's sprues,
has chickpea boils, since only he
can match the dried revithia.

Dead Parrot Boustraphedron
(for John Kinsella)

Since everything about the sea is labial
proceedings start to intends someone if
from the bay-broad creases in the sand
not is he slave a or freeborn a against
beneath you as you float in Ormos Almirou
trial the before him arrest to
to the sputum spray off the harbour wall
retain to is she divorce couple a if
if you sit and imagine Chania's horizon
half plus property her of half
perforated by successive engulfing fleets
production family's the of
as seen by one who paints his masterpiece
expose to is woman divorced a if
in certainty that its traditions will be destroyed

for staters fifty pay to is she child a

it seems that this bedraggled papagallo is
another liberates someone if child man's free a
inevitably glossal, a muted messenger
obligation an of account on
from her deep speechbox, drowned
found was he because city some from
in salt decrees and set out cruciform
man liberated the borders the of out
on the white plastic table of this beach
pays he until power his in be to is
kantina, brought to Georgioupoli
house woman's free a to goes serf a if
so as at Gortyn it may sing the code:
free be to are children their her marries and
the polis is its limits not its core

house serf's a to goes woman free a if but

just as the sea is silent in its vastest swell
action an if serfs be to are children their
best heard when it mouths the shore
judge the and won case a against brought is
like Kerouac transcribing at Big Sur
alive still are assistant his and
grey bird blown off course from Africa
witnesses as testify to are they
and dying here, just as you'd understand
right the have may moment any at anyone
what you'd repeat, mnemos of compassion
trial before arrested person a to shelter give to
where the space permits, I understand the sea.

NOTE: The law codes at Gortyn, from which the reversed sections are taken, date from around 480-450 BC, and are Europe's earliest recorded civil code. The inscription is boustraphedon (with alternating lines reversed).

Forgive the Flies

We must forgive the flies
because they are so young,
their cortices so small,
that they don't understand
what it is they crawl on.
They greet everything
like little deities:
sugar and excrement
are each as good to them.
They vomit in their nervous
pleasure and mistake
our rolled up newspapers,
suppose our dying hands
are merely waving back.

Xtapodia

The old man has come out of the sea
with flippers and mask and rubber-strung speargun.
He starts a smacking at the rocks with grey,
with a ragged handful of white and grey
like the head of a mop, speckled, splopping
on the rough back of a dark green rock;

splaying his taut legs slightly as
he bends to the task, belly round and tight
as a pony's, slapping the rock and the splop
coming between surf crashes that ebb
round his ankles. The rag resolves to two
and he's hooked them by the absence of
collarbones and smacks them against
the rock as though the rock is bad

and now I'm thinking of the swirl
of eyes and suckers on sarcophagi
embracing that rigor we pass beyond:
the loose way that Minoans inked them,
vast and bulbous like the darkness
coming at you suddenly from under

thought inside the skull-less sac
incisive as a beak yet turning
like a lock the memory of tumbling
lights like bubbles in the bloodstream
the sucker shape of light that's seen
sending eyes sideways in the skull-
dark room, the pulse that lost its shape
like a mouth relaxing from a teat

as though a murder or its neighbour
has been committed, he's rubbing, between
a swirling and that real attack
of stains, last tension in the cells
releasing into elasticity –
he's scrubbing at the rock, but the rock is clean.

The Sunglasses

A little pissed and ready for a sleep
I waded out into a broil of bay
to have a pee while nobody was near
at which the Greek kids all plunged out to play
although the waves were shoulder-high and fierce.

I turned to greet them and I saw my daughter
returning from the pool and looking mad
because I had refused to swim before
and as she splashed towards us one great scad
of crest engulfed me in its silent maw

and carried off my perfect fifties specs,
my Raybans with prescription lenses that
I never should have worn in such a tempest –
we simultaneously reached out but
the best sunglasses passed her by and left.

I roamed the foaming shallows and I searched
the labyrinths of rockpools for an hour
and found the little pencil I had perched
behind my ear. My specs had disappeared
completely as Eurydice and now

they lie beneath the bay like half a crab
and gaze up through the great Aegean's lens;
they can't tell sunlit fish from shoals of stars,
are crossed by glass-case boats and now and then,
not knowing they are watched, a swimmer flies
across my poor sunglasses' pearly sky.

Omnia Mundi Fumus et Umbra

(Inscription on a portico in Argyropouli)

I found I'd noted half a story down,
the other paper lost in other heaps
as distant as papyrus: how in a town
where a Roman infant's coffin formed the step
into church, where the great Venetian lord
agreed to marry off his daughter to
the rebel's son; how on their whispered words
these fathers' words hung – what the daughter knew
or felt was not recorded, but her name
was Sofia, wisdom, and Da Molin's wine
removed her from three hundred rebels' minds...
and there it ends. If Petros' fate was grim
and if his bride shared in it, we can't follow.
Only their motto's left, all smoke and shadows.

Karagiozis

Tonight we hear the Karagiozis man
barking his lines out in the village square,
and I imagine all the children staring
at that bright sheet on which his puppets dance:
the shadow of a hovel facing down
the shadow of a castle, and between,
the pasha strutting and the clever clown,
'Dark Eyes' in Turkish, but in these daft scenes
moustachioed and Cretan, conquering all:
the rat, the guard, the serpent. Unlike Punch
he shadows forth a history, though without
the risings, hangings, martyrdoms. His hunch
holds those. We listen to the children yell
out in the night, and hear the shadow shout.

The heat and I lie down and can't relax.
I'm thinking of that drive two years ago,
the night when I forget to buy Metaxa
and all the hairpin bends are still too new.
It feels like following the flexing float
of wire coathangers dangling each from each,
the first one hooked into the moon's ripe peach.
It feels like driving up a cat-snake's throat
and then emerging in a gale of song:
the white sail stretches, caught in this loud storm
outside the old sag-doored cafenion;
the puppet, with his concertina arm
extended, leads them all into the chorus.
We stop and watch him wobble out of focus.

We strain but can't translate his old routines:
the light that casts them seems too far away.
I turn to glance at all the kids, defined
against white plastic seats, caught by the play;
and see that on the pavements' whitewash jaws
the whole of Broiniero is perched – the men
in black and camouflage, moustache and grin,
who'd cut a sheep's throat as we passed that morning;

behind them mothers and their mothers dressed
in denser black; the question mark white crooks
of tight-lipped elders; and Pyrgos Alidaki,
the Janissary tower, behind the eldest.
And from the shadows then my father slips
a bottle into my forgotten grip.

Cockcrow

You wake me as they've just begun to cry,
returning from the loo and letting in
to our flawed net some biting thing, and then
stretch out your back's peach-fuzz passivity.
We are each other's other, alien
as fruit from meat, and yet our bodies lie
in morning's silent dialogue: do men
and women like it when their worlds collide?
Since you won't wake and I can't sleep
I listen to the mountain's hoarse old chorus,
consider how they're not quite man's rude metonym:
having no parts to stand for (far too ripe
a pun) the whole, instead each farmyard Horus
himself is that part rising like a hymn.

Cicada

Little gripper, stubborn bull
so used to clinging that you can't
shake him from your finger,
blunderer in midnight rooms
in search of china he could handle
but not lift
kri kri

Always dusty, dry-winged rattler
aged prawn-eyed Lothario
clinger to his one-tone washboard
dessicated Orpheus
always summoning his game old lover
with the opening syllable of much
kri kri

He embraces rusting vinepoles
and old beams in lieu
of cypress vine and olive bark
he gathers in arrythmic choruses
to gasp out love songs
fried up in relentless mornings
kri kri

deafener of hillsides
his paratrooper brethren hang
and rasp for recognition
his cloud of knife-sharpeners
start and fail in drifts like sand
in evening his sinister cogs give out
till nudged by one last lust

kri kri

Old Woman Up a Fodder Tree

As though blown there by a hand grenade
like the deaths you saw of grandmothers
when men you knew who now are bones
lay bleeding into olive groves –
purges like the Turks of neighbours
those women saw again, and died.

As we turn the bend for the first of many
like pins filling a young girl's hair
that's frizzing before the Easter feast
we see you picking leaves for beasts,
another alphabet's black shape
we glance at but we can't read plainly

so strand you shaded up that tree
as though we drew four crow-like dots
then spilt the ink in joining them,
as though you'd drop upon a lamb
like some fantastic attercop,
as though descending meant some fee.

Is there a currency for loss of face?
The dead would know who we should pay,
since we can't translate what we expose –
that covered hair, these wrinkled clothes –
back to your proper dignity,
we feed our urgency, and pass.

Walnut

Between a lemon and an apple hangs
the walnut's fruit, far lighter than it looks,
aware that lacquer carvings, a netsuke
egg, fold within it like the tree's new tongue.

You cut into the green rind and it smells
of leather; juice clings to your fingers, slick
and hard to wash off. Leave the inner shell
to dry on concrete like a drunk maracca.

Then there's the cracking to achieve without
crushing the dry freight half-embalmed within.
But this one, found in grass, is bitter fruit,
its white frills shrink-wrapped in a blackened skin

like Wood Ear mushroom, so the walnut glows
when bared: albino coral, foetal bone.

Drosoulites

Towards the Feast of the Assumption we felt
the skin of things begin to peel away:

the cat-snake left its scratched white plastic sleeve
on the threshold of the ruined house next door,

its phantom arm still pointing at the brambles
that barrage the roofless arched interior

with thorn trajectories. One morning the ghost
of a grasshopper fell from the vine, nearly landing

in my daughter's bowl. It was complete from the hooks
in its still bent legs to the lids of the eyes,

the colour of a chickpea husk – we could see
its infant wings as though on the lapel

of a *Fallschirmjager*. After that
a whole squadron fell, hollow as uniforms.

The midnight before the Feast the dark began
to slap its heels, louder and more insistently, until

we lay there deafened as a skin of water tried
to reattach itself to everything outside.

Drosoulites: (lit.) dew-ghosts.

Emprosneros

The Cretan night compels you to believe
in thirsty spirits like the Englishman
Sofia hid beneath the platform where
Izzie now sleeps. It's in the way the vine
blots out a star-crammed sky as though you were
thrown out of time. It's in the crickets' pitch,
that high tinnitus of the hillsides like
a signal from an unseen star, the shift
between the upper valley where we lie
and those crotales now sounding out below,
their only resonance each other's note.
Wounded himself he treated the small boy
who shot himself with one of all the guns
the British dumped with helmets, rations, kit
before their forced retreat along the Gorge.
Dogs bark to keep all kinds of things at bay,
and all the cockerels mark the first false dawn.
So many ratchet out their set response
it fills the hills with that call's scrawny shapes,
a field of cartoon jacaranda, or
coral releasing fertile clouds, as though
both crest and cry made sub-aquatic sense.
You try not hearing words from each hoarse throat:
the child's notation only he would know
when everyone had fled from Sfakia.
A sheep-bell tonks, the animals confront
that other sphere with their respectful groans.

The morning hears cicadas sharpen with
the gathering of heat, each hundred notes
each virtuoso plays the same old note,
these one chord wonders build a wall of sound
through which the grumbled incantations made
into a microphone must filter if
the van that trundles through the square will sell
its vegetables or clothes or fish or chairs –
you lie and try to hear the words you know
he must be barking, but they never match.
Sometimes he sits there and blasts out canned lyre,

sometimes the church bells teach us all sustain
in four notes, and the long voice of the priest
attaches us to liturgy and year
like grappling legs on the cicadas who
are hushed now by that rarity, a cloud.

By now we're on the patio, in shade,
and looking down the valley through the slants
of lemon tree and walnut where two feet
of pale green lizard slid, and past the cactus
to red tiled roofs and whitewashed window frames,
the biscuit orange stone and room-wide arches,
the blue shade walls well-buried in the trees,
the black-eyed window of the Turkish tower –
and let the sounds depict Emprosneros.
The dogs, still querulous, still echoing,
the children, woken now and not afraid,
the voices of the men who sit in black
whenever we drive through the square, who turn
hook-handled sticks and hide in their moustaches'
grey handlebars the fifty year old feuds
that stocked these farms with aged widows and
the names of clans that fought the Nazis, fought
the Turks and fought Venetians, Romans, fought
Achaeans until Homer listed those
that fought the Trojans (who were Cretans too).
The silence from the Janissary's fort
is ground bass to these other instruments:
the last few gunshots cracking on the hills,
the starting of a saw, the stumbling tick
of chickens' panicking, unstable clocks.

Our neighbours' voices drift in with the wind:
Ireni crowdling to her hens in that
high tone that women can direct across
the valley just as easily as still
a baby; thinner-voiced, the *yeros* gives
Apostolos reports on crops he's gleaned
from the kilometre he's dragged himself
on crutches, now ensconced beneath his tree
with segments from the glut of cucumber
which we encounter as a daily gift.

From 6 A.M. the food arrives in heaps:
domates, *sikes*, *ladhi* (their own press),
kremeedhia, *melitzanes* and *avga*
and, six a day for weeks, *anguria*.
We are at war with cucumbers: we fight
them in *tzatziki*, in *salata*, meals
spent staring at the hills above the town –
the first are Silver Howe-high, with round tops
still reachable by donkey or by car,
small whitewash churches knucklebone their crests.
Behind them rise pine-speckled barer heights
that make a single Cuillin-shrinking ridge
and pull us out of Europe in their skirts.
Cypresses jag their slopes the way the boards
on which memorials are pinned in cities
collect old staples in a rusting horde.

But past these mountains, through their dipping brims,
the further higher range appears as mantles
which sit upon their shoulders, white as salt
with rice grains in it, lunar almost, quite
beyond: they look more like two glaciers
that ought to grind down smoothly over us.
They match the churches on the lower hills
to dwarf them: that containing ridge becomes
the skirts of Crete's old goddess, Britomart,
Sweet Virgin, Mistress of the Labyrinth –
the Lefka Ori are her face, Diktynna,
the Queen of Beasts, seen on the heights between
two lions, Serpent Goddess – if these are
her names, and anyone Minoan stood
here ever, looking up, as in safe moments
perhaps he did, their hidden Englishman
or Brit, an officer or other rank,
abandoned to his wound and to this speech,
this acre, this consuming mounting heat.

One afternoon when any drop in wind
sprang sweat on every limb and upper lip,
when in the anti-small hours people dozed
and I translated Celsius into
the more familiar Fahrenheit, I heard

come rising up from somewhere in the village
a lyre going round and round a tune
too many times to be recorded and
too well for practice, and I wondered if
he heard this too, through fevers and the skill
that knew he wouldn't heal for want of care
no one could risk their families to give.
The song announced its core in lazy tones
that almost undermined the mood it had
been built to hold, and said a sulky fear
was all the hand could summon in this heat
at how our lives are suddenly withheld
from us, a childishness that made things worse.

Apostolos announces evening by
censing tomatoes big as breasts with squirts
from the flamethrower-shaped weedkiller kit
we rescued from the donkey shed: he moves
in gasmask in between his heavy yield
and light begins to change. The bleaching out
is weakened and the grain of things stands up,
the intimacies of concrete and leaves,
as though light was a drug. You're heavier, tired,
aware the distant slopes have bloodstreams, guts.
They're almost as translucent as cicadas
whose clockwork strikes begin to drop away,
tin monkeys with tin drums. The adult night
is band on band of tints resisting names:
the valley arcs its back and takes the bruise,
its air's ribs turn through yellow, mauve and grey
as though interrogated by the dark.
You feel night as a loss as colour fails
and trees give up their depths for silhouettes.
They tried to carry him to Vamos in
the last ditch of this same concealing gloom
and somewhere on the staggered way he died.
We sent them a citation in the peace.
Two weeks before young Nikos came back home
from Athens with his kids and told us this,
one night when Debbie drove my parents to
Georgioupoli, I came out of the kitchen
and almost leaning in the doorway was

the scent of pipe tobacco – probably
Apostolos's drifting cigarette.
Then Izzie found the tamper in the drawer
without me telling her this trace and said,
'Perhaps this was the Englishman's.' In these
half-incoherent tokens we dissolve.

The crickets' glass harmonica restarts,
two treefrogs boop each other like wee subs:
I wander to the gate to watch the owl
land on that stave of five electric wires
the poles notate between our modal homes,
its white sol-fa that silently departs
to shriek above my head. And music comes
as I lean in the metre-deep old doorway
and listen as a shield bug's buzz up here
is picked up by a motor bike down there:
children kept up too late still chatter on
and the cafenion's cantors still recount
how I will never be at home here. Yet,
while Debbie puts her earplugs in, I wait,
try to translate these slant approaches to
a stillness which conceals the motion of
the stars. I look up through the vine at how
they like to glint between the leaves, at how
the constellations hang in clusters, how
the galaxy itself is hanging like
a vine, its darkest branches resting on
these unseen mountain tops. I lean the way
the Englishman once did, until it's time
to go back to my family and sleep.

ACKNOWLEDGEMENTS

Acknowledgements are due to the editors of the following publications in which some of these poems first appeared: *Fulcrum, Literaturen Vestnik, Poetry Review, The Rialto* and *The Times Literary Supplement*. Several poems from 'Over the Wall' were commissioned by ARTS UK as part of their 'Writing on the Wall' project. 'A Midsummer Light's Nighthouse', 'Macaroni Pie Fetish', 'Ode to the Old Tay Bridge', 'McPelvis Meddley' and 'Ode to Freedom' were all the results of commissions by BBC Radio 3 and the World Service: special thanks to Tim Dee, Ian McMillan and Julian May. 'A Midsummer Light's Nighthouse', 'Sailors Home' and 'Shanty of the Sailors' Moon' all appeared in *Sailor's Home*, edited by Yang Lian (Shearsman Books, 2005). 'Sofia City Blues' and 'Tissue Remains' appeared in *Magnetic North*, edited by Claire Malcolm (New Writing North, 2006).

   I would like to thank the British Council for the invitations and the hospitality which made many of these poems possible, in particular Debanjan Chakrabarti, Sarika Chaudhuri, Leah Davcheva, Tatyana Ilyina, Rathi Jafer and Elena Uniskova. Thanks also to Julian Forrester, Polly Clark, the Scottish Arts Council and Cove Park Artists Centre, as well as to Zhang Wei and Wansongpu Writers Centre, for the Poet to Poet project which gave rise to 'Lost Films'. Especial thanks to Claire Malcolm and Anna Summerford at New Writing North, and to Linda Anderson of Newcastle University, for all their support.